plant
parenthood
for
urban gardeners

kate staples

illustrations by kevin o'malley

MACMILLAN • USA

MACMILLAN
A Simon & Schuster Macmillan Company
1633 Broadway
New York, NY 10019

MACMILLAN is a registered trademark of Macmillan, Inc.

Library of Congress Cataloging-in-Publication Data
Staples, Kate.
Plant parenthood for urban gardeners / Kate Staples: illustrations by
    Kevin O'Malley.
        p. cm.
    Includes index.
    ISBN 0-02-861916-1 (pbk.)
    1. Gardening. 2. Container gardening. I. Title.
SB453.S665 1997   635.9'65—dc21
97-14557   CIP

Manufactured in the United States of America

10 9 8 7 6 5 4 3 2 1

Book design by Nick Anderson

For my mother, Emily Anne Tuttle, my sister, Missy, and my brothers Tom and Greg, and in memory of my father, Loring Staples, Jr.

contents

*I bought a few houseplants and watched them
all suffer a slow, agonizing death.*

introduction

If you've picked up this book, chances are you've spent most of your life taking green things for granted, assuming that—at least for decorative purposes—they're basically interchangeable with your great-grandmother Heloise's tin candlesticks or a bowl of plastic fruit. The only real difference is that plants demand more than an occasional dusting, and when they keel over, make your mother's guilt trips seem low-key.

Maybe now your nesting instinct is kicking in and you've decided it's time to take responsibility for something living: something that doesn't need a litter-box change or five daily walks; something that won't throw up in your shoes, but inspires a confidence you haven't experienced since your chia pet sprouted.

When it comes to calming influences, plants can be like an hour of yoga, two Valium, and an hour's worth of infomercials all wrapped up in a terra-cotta pot. Especially after one of those Anacin days, nothing beats the surge of omnipotence you feel noting that little Fern is all grown up or that the comatose geranium you rescued from the garbage woke up and churned out a new bud.

The all-too-common flip side is the demoralizing sensation of seeing your little life form go belly up. You tried everything, from dousing it with a case of Perrier to serenading it with a sotto voce chorus of "Muskrat Love" and still it looks like your prom carnation after the all-night party. Maybe you scanned one of the gardening guides currently on the market, but when you realized the index was a litany of Latin you were forced into a cold sweat by a flashback to your seventh-grade anatomy exam.

How is this book different? Well, first of all, I too have spent most of my life avoiding plants like the plague. I've feigned allergies to chlorophyll and panicked when people brought me cut flowers. A few years ago, when the nurturing gene kicked in, I bought a few houseplants and watched them all suffer a slow and agonizing death while I frantically flipped through books and wondered how it was possible that my parents had passed me the acne gene but hoarded the gardening one.

Nothing against all those gardening tomes out there, but the vast majority are wildly boring unless you're the type who wants to know that a geranium is also known as *Pelargonium × hortorum* or would seriously consider keeping a container of cow manure in your apartment for the good of the greenery. This book is for the rest of us—those looking for something to cover the water stain on the windowsill or who want to dazzle former college roommates with our newfound nurturing abilities. Maybe someday you will get that gardening bug and turn your living room into an arboretum, but in the meantime you need to know that low light does not mean crammed in the back of the closet under your abdominal cruncher.

There doesn't have to be too much more to it. Repotting, pruning, and pinching are all occasional herbal obligations, but owning a plant doesn't have to induce more angst than it alleviates. No matter how inept you are at nurturing, there is a plant out there for you, one so hardy you'd pretty much have to go out of your way to kill it. And better yet, you don't need English subtitles to unearth it.

Kate Staples

chapter one

Horticulture 101

Green Room Basics

When you get to a certain point in life, it's assumed that you've caught on to the basic domestic coping terms and suddenly, it's too late to ask anyone what they mean for fear you'll sound foolish. Along the lines of "poaching" in the kitchen, these are the particulars plant people toss around.

Annual: A plant that will generally live for only one season. Many of the flowers you see in window boxes—impatiens, petunias, pansies, and nasturtiums, for example—are annuals.

Biennial: Those with a two-year life span. The first year, they produce only leaves, the second year they flower, then they die. Forget-me-nots and foxgloves are biennials.

Perennial: As the name implies, these plants will stick around for a while, enduring through the winter and into the next year, as long as you remember to water them.

Bulb: Sort of like a compressed plant, a bulb is usually pear-shaped and has all the equipment for an amazing flower packed inside. Tulips, paper whites, amaryllis, and daffodils are all grown from bulbs. Corms and tubers are basically the same thing, only in different shapes.

Bud: Sort of like an embryo, it's a little saclike growth that sticks off the side of a stem and contains the flower or leaf.

Cutting: A piece of a leaf or stem you cut off the plant and stick in water or soil until it grows roots and turns into a baby version of the mother plant.

Deciduous: The opposite of evergreen, these plants lose their leaves at the end of their growth period and grow new ones after their rest period.

Dormancy: Just like you need that occasional all-sleep weekend, plants go into "leave-me-alone" periods where the rate of growth slows considerably and they need less light and water. Most plants will kick into their dormant period in the fall, with changes in light and temperature.

Forcing: Using artificial means, like temperature or light, to make plants grow and flower before they would naturally.

Hardy: A hardy plant can survive through the frost period of a specific zone.

Node: The point on the stem where leaves grow, also called a joint.

Rhizome: Like an underground stem, it produces its own root system and acts as a food-storage system for the plant.

Seedling: A plant in its infancy, usually just after it has popped out of the soil. It consists of either a skinny stem and two little leaflike protrusions at the top or a miniature version of the adult plant.

Tender: The opposite of hardy, a tender plant is one that is especially sensitive to cold temperatures.

Topdress: An alternative to repotting, topdressing refers to adding a layer of new soil, generally after removing the same amount of old soil.

Variegated: Whereas most leaves are green (duh), variegated leaves contain more than one color, whether different shades of green or combinations of colors like yellow, red, purple, or white.

Zone: The United States is divided into numbered growing zones depending on factors like average temperature and frost date; gardening magazines and catalogs usually match plant descriptions with a listing of what zones they are best suited for. However, this is more of a concern for outdoor gardening.

Light

One of the most confusing aspects of plant parenthood is figuring out where your charges should live. Most plants you buy are marked with some sort of lighting instructions, but discerning between low light and filtered light and part shade is one of those "huh?" experiences.

Basically, "low light" means no direct sunlight. Place your plant at the back of a sunny room or near a north-facing window, where it will soak up the available rays without leaf-scorching brightness. "Full sun" means pretty much just that, a lot of direct sunlight, preferably at least five hours a day.

Then there are other light-related terms that seem designed to confuse, such as "reflected light" or "filtered light." The former refers to sunlight bounced off another source, such as that glass monstrosity across the street or the white apartment house next door; the latter is direct light that has passed through a sheer shade or other filter.

Pruning

Left to their own devices, most rapidly growing plants would end up looking lanky and strung out. By pruning, or cutting back on the ends, you can fashion it into whatever shape you want, from Lyle Lovett to Don King. You can use your fingers, a scissors, or a pruner. Some people prefer the natural feel of fingers, while others prefer a pruner so they can avoid spending the rest of the day trying to dig the sap from under their fingernails. If you use a duller instrument, you risk crushing the stem, which will lead to the plant version of gangrene and eventually, a dead limb.

The best time to prune is during the active growing season, which generally means spring and summer. This is when the plant is best equipped to compensate for its lost limbs and send out more shoots. If you begin snipping when it's resting, there's a smaller likelihood that new growth will replace what you've cut away.

First of all, stand back and take a good look at your plant.

First of all, stand back and take a good look at your plant. Decide whether you want to drastically change the shape or just clip back the ragged ends. Though plants don't generally get embarrassed by bad clip jobs, keep in mind that you're going to have to live with the results for a while so go easy on it. When you cut back a stem, do it just below a node, which is the spot from which a leaf grows. The plant will compensate by sending two or more shoots from the spot so you'll end up with a bushier finish. One basic rule is if you want a bushy specimen, pinch the stems near the top of the plant, as this will cause it to fill in on the sides. For a more statuesque shape, trim back the side shoots.

When you're dealing with flowers, pruning becomes much more important. You want to keep the flowers alive as long as possible as well as force out as many blooms as you can. "Pinching back" is a way to force out more flowers from a stem. As stupid as it sounds, pinching back the first flower—by snipping it just below the next node down—will basically piss the plant off and encourage it to send out more buds. Once the flowers are past their prime, you should "deadhead" (pinch the flower back the way you would a live one) a gruesome-sounding but important way to make the plant look nicer and preserve its energy for more growth.

When you've got a variegated plant, pinch off any all-green shoots, since they are quick to reproduce and can overwhelm an otherwise multicolor plant with a green invasion.

The Right Match

Before you go falling in love with the first little green thing you see, you should take a few things into consideration. Plants have some basic needs and if you try to fudge on them, you'll probably end up with a brown mess and a guilt trip.

Exposure

There's a good reason many plants end up on the windowsill—it's where they'll get the most sunlight. Of course, depending on the plant and where the window faces, that could be a bad thing. Unless you live in the Southern Hemisphere, you're not going to squeeze a lot of direct sunlight out of a window with northern exposure, so steer clear of sun-thirsty plants in that location. By the same token, a shade-loving plant will soon look like a barbecue victim if it's plopped in a window with southern exposure.

Figure out where you want to keep your plant and make note of how much light that spot gets throughout the day. If it's a dark corner, your options are more limited and you should avoid plants that need lots of direct sunlight or you'll end up with a sad and straggly stem. Keep in mind when you go shopping that all but the most temperamental plants can survive, and even flourish, in less than perfect conditions. With most plants you can fudge a little— a few hours short of the standard six sunny hours is probably not going to make too much of a difference. When in doubt, ask your friendly plant salesperson. If you really want to cheat nature and set up a light-thirsty plant in a dark room, check into artificial lighting (see page 14).

Water

Yes, all plants need water, even cacti. Some need dramatically less water, but every plant needs some, so if you're in severe responsibility denial stick with plastic daisies. If you're going to take the plunge, so to speak, consider how often you're going to remember (or be home) to water it. Frequent travelers gone weeks at a time are better off with a more self-sufficient bloomer, such as a geranium or philodendron, which can hold on to an ample supply of its own water to endure days of neglect. Compulsive types might want a species more difficult to drown.

There are other watering methods, besides conscientious neighbors, for vacationing plant owners (see tip), but again, you and your plant are going to be happier with a realistic match.

TIP: Long-Term Watering

Whether you're a frequent traveler or just forgetful, you can keep your plant in the H_2O between trips to the faucet. All you have to do is set up a wick, sort of an IV between the plant and a bowl of water. Old pantyhose or cotton shoelaces will work fine; just stick one end a few inches into the soil and put the other end in a large bowl of water. The plant will suck up nourishment as it needs it.

TIP: Water Works

This is the question every new plant person wants to ask but doesn't, for fear of sounding like a complete idiot: How much water are you supposed to give it anyway? It's not such a dumb question, really. How often you water a plant is going to depend on the plant itself, something you should find out when you buy it. If you water it too often, you're going to rot the roots and condemn it to a slow and ugly death, so you're better off erring on the dry side. But as for how much water to give it, again each plant has different needs—but all occasionally need a good dousing, where you saturate the soil so even the bottom tier of roots gets nourishment. If water comes through the bottom, you've accomplished that goal and more. Let the water sit in the tray for a few minutes; if the plant soaks it back up, it was thirsty; if not, it's sated and you should pour out the excess water.

Humidity

Unless you live in the desert, you'll recognize humidity as that thing that makes a bad hair day even worse. Basically, humidity is moisture in the air and to most plants, some form of it is essential. A quick Botany 101: Plants have tons of pores on their leaves that they open wide to suck up nutrients in the air, losing water in the process. The more water that's in the air, the less the plant forfeits.

A lot of plant ailments stem from lack of humidity. Moisture-deprived plants suffer a slow and pathetic demise: leaves whither up and drop off, flower buds shrivel, and flowers die premature deaths.

That doesn't mean you have to create a hotbox in your home—depending on where you live, your climate might be humid enough. But if your plant is looking really sad, there's a possibility that its leaves are dehydrated. Spritzing it with water is one way to give it an instant infusion, but you'd have to spritz regularly for your plant to benefit. If you're the type who barely remembers to pour some water in the soil a few times a week, this is probably not going to work.

A more reasonable idea is to provide humidity from below. Put a layer of pebbles, a brick, or a chunk of wood on a tray and fill the tray with water until it's just below the top of the pebbles (or brick or block) and put the plant on top of it. The water will evaporate into the air and create the humidity the plant needs to perk up.

Yet another option is to buy a humidifier. Though obviously not a viable option in windowsill gardening, a humidifier placed in the general vicinity (though preferably not on top of) your indoor plants will keep them moist and help them hold water, meaning fewer visits with the watering can.

TIP: Some Generalities

Perhaps a true devotee can tell from a glance what a plant's basic needs are; the rest of us need it spelled out. There are a few general rules that can guide you in care and feeding. Fat stems and thick leaves, for example are a sign that the plant needs more infrequent watering and is less reliant on high humidity. Thin leaves and stems are more likely to beg frequent water infusions, as are large plants in smaller containers.

(continues)

(continued)

Plants with thick, waxy leaves probably don't like too much direct sunlight, while those with variegated leaves demand more to keep the foliage bright. During their rest periods, most plants can make do with less intense light for shorter periods of time.

Soil

This is one of those things that turn real gardeners into fanatics. Everyone, it seems has some secret mix of ingredients—one quarter little white things, one quarter cow manure, one quarter dead moldy stuff, one quarter other puffy white things—which they're quite certain will create results to drive the next-door neighbor into paroxysms of envy. Personally, I don't have the time or patience to pour bags of smelly and dirty stuff out onto my kitchen table, mix it up, and pack it lovingly around little Bud. The truth is that for basic planting, a big old bag of soil mix will do just fine. You can find it at the hardware store, the grocery store, or the local plant nursery. Most contain a mix of stuff like vermiculite (little puffy white things) to keep the soil light, plus various nutrients.

Not a good idea is a big chunk of dirt you've scooped out of the local park or the next-door neighbor's yard. Plants need some sort of nutrition and dirt that's been kicked around by kids and peed on by dogs will not do the trick.

Food

Yet another hotbed of gardening controversy. By most accounts, you really should use some sort of fertilizer occasionally, since the plant isn't getting nutrition from any other source. But the questions are: which to use, how much, and how often? As a sort of ugly scientific experiment, I've studiously avoided feeding some of my hardier plants, including a philodendron and a rubber plant

Everyone, it seems, has some secret mix.

and both are doing just fine after three years of fertilizer-free existence. Still, it is a good idea to toss in some plant food once in a while, especially for flowering plants.

Check out the labels of your basic foods. There should be three numbers—15-30-15, for example. The first number refers to the amount of nitrogen, which promotes healthy leaves; the second is phosphorous, for flowers; the third is potassium, for all-around health and happiness. Basic fertilizers like Miracle-Gro, will do just fine for most plants, and according to an informal survey of experts, you don't need special food for your African violets.

TIP: Naptime

Like humans, plants need a break at the end of a long spurt of working. Humans take a vacation, plants take a rest period. The time of year depends on the plant. Many go through active growth periods in the spring and summer then go dormant in fall, others do the opposite. You'll know, of course, because the growth period is when your plant is producing new leaves and flowers. During that period, fertilize more frequently so your plant has the energy to produce. While it's resting, usually in the winter, lay off on the food and water a little less frequently.

TIP: Almost-Free Fertilizer

A couple of ways to pamper your plants with minimum cash outlay:

- Save the water you use to boil eggs, and use it to water your plants (after it cools, of course). The calcium and other minerals are great for growth.
- Dissolve Epsom salts in the water you use to feed plants. It won't replace fertilizer, but it's high in nutrients and will give them a boost.

Tricks of the Trade

Tools

While you most definitely don't need six different kinds of scissors and a raft of hoes, a couple of appropriate tools will make your life easier, your fingernails stronger, and your flatware sharper.

Pruner: The most essential, this looks kind of like a cross between a wrench and a scissors, and is used to shape and liberate the plant from dead ends. You could try to use regular scissors or your fingers, but they won't make as clean a break and will wear out more quickly. A decent pruner shouldn't cost more than ten bucks; you could go the fancy route if you want, but those tools are geared toward someone with more than two plants. Look for one with rubber hand grips for better control. A pair that has some sort of locking mechanism is also a good idea, especially if you have a child or the coordination of one.

Watering can: Again, not an essential, but it tends to give you more control than your coffee cup or an old beer can. Other than aesthetics, there's not much of a difference between high- and low-end versions, but it's a good idea to pick up one with a removable spray nozzle so you can opt for either a fine spray or a steady stream over the base of the plant.

Spray bottle: The schools of thought on misting are diverse, but the general consensus is that it can do no harm. Plants also need humidity, and an occasional misting of water can help deliver that. Misting can also clean off the leaves and wash away the random pest. Any kind of bottle will do—a cheap drugstore brand or even a (well-washed) recycled bottle from window cleaner.

Chopsticks: For plants that need support, like tomatoes or peppers, chopsticks can do the trick. Just stick them in the dirt next to the main stem and strap them together with string or one of those twisty things you use with plastic bags.

Fake Florida

The horticultural equivalent of sending your plants to winter in Florida, artificial light is a pretty self-explanatory term connoting an owner-imposed and controlled setup. It's a little more ambitious, but a great way to defy the gods of window exposure. There are a number of different ways to go about creating an indoor sun factory. The easiest and least effective is to use household lamps and incandescent bulbs. The problem is that these bulbs emit at least 70 percent of their energy in the form of heat, so there's a solid likelihood you'll scorch your plants' leaves if you set them up too close. But at too far a distance they aren't strong enough to do a whole lot of good.

Fluorescent tubes are a much better bet. Many gardening catalogs will sell the whole fluorescent-tube setup, but that can cost in the hundreds of dollars. Hardware stores will sell basically the same thing for a fraction of the cost. All you need is the casing, either attached to chains for hanging—from hooks in the wall, for example—or with mounting apparatus on the top so you can attach it to an overhang, like the underside of a shelf. Slightly less attractive but even easier to deal with is the type that comes with its own adjustable legs, allowing you to set it up pretty much anywhere you choose. The beauty of this type of lighting is that you can now set up a full garden in the closet if that's your pleasure, and enjoy it while you change your socks. Better yet, go for a dark living room or your bedroom, or mount a lighting unit to the underside of a kitchen cabinet and line up a row of plants on the counter below it. Few household sights are more impressive than a pot of bright flowers popping out from the middle of a dark room.

Not all fluorescent bulbs are alike, however. Different types are geared toward specific light spectra. The most important light components for plant growth are red and blue-violet. Look for a bulb labeled specifically for plant growth, or pick out a wide-spectrum tube, which is especially good for needy specimens. The other alternative is to pick up a fixture that takes two bulbs and combine different types, one with more red light, the other high in blue-violet. No matter which spectrum you choose, keep the wattage on the low side—somewhere around 40 watts is usually sufficient. It is important to give your plants some rest and cooling-out time. Unless you want to be a diligent light sentry, you should also invest in a timer that will click the bulbs on and off, on a schedule you'll decide after a few weeks' of trial and error. Anywhere from twelve to eighteen hours of illumination a day is a good starting point. Check the plants daily for any signs that you'll need to make an adjustment. If the leaves are fading out or looking droopy, you might need to up the dosage; with any sign of drying out, you should adjust their schedule and leave them in the dark a bit longer.

Placement over the plants is key, and takes a little experimentation. Optimum distance from light to leaf will also vary depending on the type of plant and where it is in the growing cycle. In general, nonflowering plants need less intense exposure, a good rule of thumb being a distance of one to two feet from the top of the plant to the bulb. Harder workers in general, flowering plants need some more intense help, and should be placed from one foot to no less than six inches away from the bulb. Dealing with both types under one light can be as simple as stacking the containers on coasters to bring them closer to the lamp.

Monitor the plants regularly for hints that they might need some realignment. Signs that they're too close and need a break include stunted growth and scorched leaves. Understimulation is indicated by leggy branches (spindly stems with leaves placed far apart) and falling leaves. Adjust the plant three inches up or down, depending on its needs, and give it another week before reevaluating. It's going to take a few months for the plant to really settle into its new routine so be patient. When it begins to look happy, you've successfully faked it out.

This type of lighting arrangement is especially good for growing seeds and cuttings, since the babies tend to be particularly demanding. Just be sure you adjust the distance from the light as they grow.

Cleanliness is a big virtue in the land of artificial light; a dusty bulb will be substantially dimmer so wipe away the excess dirt and lint periodically.

A Breath of Fresh Air

Just like you or your goldfish, plants need a lot of fresh air to maintain their good looks and health. This is especially important to remember in artificial lighting situations, like basements or closets where a fresh breeze is an unknown commodity. As long as it won't dramatically alter the temperature in the room, a cracked window is a good way to ventilate. If there's no window or if you're in the midst of a deep freeze, a fan will do the trick. Make sure it's at a setting and distance that will cause the air to circulate gently without providing tornado conditions.

Hot Spots

As previously mentioned, gardening magazines and catalogs usually display plant descriptions along with a listing of what zones they are best suited for. The zones refer to areas of the country and their climates, but in houseplants it's not such a big factor because you have a pretty large element of control over the conditions. The inside of a Floridian's home is not likely to be all that much different from a Minnesotan's, other than the amount of shag carpeting and pastel furniture.

Most houseplants prefer a temperature between 65 to 75°F, though they will tolerate a variance of a few degrees higher or lower. A slight drop in nighttime temperatures, from 5 to 10 degrees, is normal, and actually good for the plant. Dramatic drops in temperature—especially for extended periods of time— are not a good idea for almost any plant, though there are some, such as desert cacti, which actually prefer it.

When you're deciding where to put your plant, keep in mind that there are danger zones, like bad neighborhoods, where the mortality rate is high. A sunny window, for example, is a great spot in the summer, but a chill factory when it's cold and snowy outside. Steam radiators and vents can provide much needed humidity in the winter, but can also send up too much heat and can scorch and dry out the leaves. The stove is another spot to avoid.

Settling In

Finding a Home

The beauty of plant adoption is that you can plop it in a standard terra-cotta pot or you can get creative with your choice of container. If you comb through the local nursery, chances are you'll come up with options ranging in price from a couple of bucks for plastic to several hundred for a more artistic creation.

Far be it from me to attempt a Martha Stewart moment, but you don't have to ante up a fortune or fire up a kiln to come up with an original container. Brush some water-based paint on a standard plastic or terra-cotta pot or rub it with sandpaper to create a weathered veneer. Found objects can be some of the best—not to mention least expensive— options: an old watering can, a miniature wheelbarrow, your high school mug, a beer can, a beheaded Barbie. The only requirements are that it's somewhat watertight (if you don't want a muddy windowsill) and has drainage holes. It is possible to get by without the holes, but you'll have to fill the bottom at least an inch or so with rocks or shards from the clay pot the cat broke, and still pay special attention to your watering habits. Otherwise you're likely to drown the poor thing by forcing it to sit in a wading pool.

You can create drainage holes by drilling at the bottom of the container. Just make sure the holes are big enough for water to escape or you'll end up with rotted roots and a plant that looks more like a winter tree branch. If you use wood or some other not-exactly-watertight material, line it with plastic so it doesn't rot away (but make sure you poke drainage holes in the plastic as well). Put a saucer or other receptacle underneath to catch any drainage.

The type of material you use—wood, terra-cotta, plastic, ceramic, or metal—will affect how well it holds liquid and, therefore, your responsibilities as water bearer. Both wood and terra-cotta tend to absorb water so you'll be called on to replenish your plant's supply more often. Plastic is impermeable to just about anything and will keep the moisture contained longer so you'll be less beholden to feeding times. Other non-porous materials, such as ceramic and tin, are similar to plastic in their water retention.

Be creative when matching plant to container. As long as you leave enough space for the root structure, a big bushy plant can be an attention-grabber when it's overwhelming a smaller container. Some trailers, like ivy, create a surprising visual impact when seen spilling out of a tall urn.

TIP: The All-Purpose Container

When in doubt about the merging of container, plant, and the decor of your home, go with simple terra-cotta. The color is neutral, so it looks good in every scenario, plus the pots tend to look better with age. A few years of chipped edges and faded spots will make it look like a prized possession.

TIP: Conservation Efforts

Plants in small pots tend to dry out more quickly. If you feel as if you spend more time dealing with your plant's thirst than your own, there are a couple of quick fixes. One is to put your small pot inside a larger one. Buy even more time by filling the space between the pots with damp peat moss, then sprinkle pebbles on top. There's also the possibility that the plant is telling you something, like perhaps it's strangling in this tiny pot and it's time to move it into larger quarters (see Chapter 2).

Leafy Furniture

There are several ways you can use flowers and greenery to spice up your living space. Trees and other big plants can double as room dividers, for example, as could a large trellis and fast-growing ivy. For a more seasonal feeling in the summer, replace your fireplace screen with a bushy plant.

Line a viewless window with shelves and fill it up with little plants. Sometimes a grouping of greenery—with foliage of different shapes and sizes—can make the dullest space look infinitely more interesting.

The only real rule of decorating with plants is to be daring; no matter how odd an arrangement looks, it can always be moved around.

Hang On

There was a period of time where hanging plants were considered a litmus test of good taste—you hang, you fail. Now, as long as you don't go suspending them over your lava lamps, hanging plants can be perky addition to a blah wall or window. The catch is that you need to put extra thought into the accoutrements.

Avoid the white plastic pots in which many traditional hanging plants are sold. From the bottom, which is what you'll be looking at, they look like cheap white plastic pots. You need something lightweight but attractive—heavy-duty stone is probably out of the question. Wood pots and smaller terra-cotta containers are easy to hang and pleasant on the eyes; look for ready-to-hang versions with predrilled holes or hooks for suspension. Otherwise, you'll have to rig it up yourself using eyelets or hooks specially designed for the pots. Wire or chain suspensions tend to be the most attractive and functional support systems, and pay attention to the hook you use to anchor the plant—brass and wrought-iron are the kinds of touches that will convert the formerly anti-hangers. Just make sure the whole system is sturdy so you don't end up with an Elmer Fudd–size lump on your head when you least expect it.

Crucial to the whole effect is the type of plant you choose. Obviously, the very upright are not going to provide a great deal of pleasure for those with an ant's-eye view. Traditional picks are those with trailing leaves, like ivy, spider plants, and philodendrons, all of which are good choices. You could also be a little adventurous, hanging the container a bit lower and filling it with a mishmash of different plants (with similar light and water requirements) or even a few cacti.

Those new to hanging plants might be in for a surprise come watering time. If you've got holes in the bottom you risk an unexpected indoor shower. To avoid drenching the antique carpet, you could either include a drainage dish underneath the pot (easiest if it's the type of hanging system that wraps under the pot), stand by with a dish to catch the overflow, water it just enough to nourish the soil, or take it down and water it in the sink, returning it when it's fully drained. A pretty good compromise, if you don't choose the suspended dish route, is to water it a bit more sparingly and every few weeks or so give it the sink treatment.

*Just make sure the whole system is sturdy so you don't end up
with an Elmer Fudd–size lump on your head.*

Keep in mind that since plants reach for the light, your hanging greenery is going to grow toward the window. If you want a well-balanced, somewhat symmetrical appearance, you're going to have to rotate it every few weeks.

Support System

Feeling blue-blooded? If you want to create the impression of an ivy league apartment, you can accomplish it fairly easily by using a quick-growing climbing species and a trellis. Though ivy is particularly famous for its climbing capabilities, you can use other plants such as jasmine, wandering Jew, and purple heart.

Trellises can be found at local plant or home stores, or you can make your own out of gathered sticks or bamboo shoots wired together in whatever shape you choose—a grid, a heart, an abstract design. Make sure you leave ends that are long enough to secure in the pot. Most of these climbers need little encouragement; simply wrap stems around the trellis and they'll pull a boa constrictor act on it, worming their way around any available space. In order to get the configuration you want, you might have to help it along a bit and gently steer the stems in the right direction.

Trellises are a perfect way to shove the proverbial dirt under the rug. A window with a bad view, a drab corner, a stained wall—you can solve many decorating dilemmas with a well-placed trellis and a quick-growing plant.

chapter two

Ready, Set, Grow

Natural Birth vs. Adoption

Once you've decided to take the plunge and raise a living green being, you have a few more decisions to make. Sure, you could grab the first plant you see at the supermarket checkout line, but you'd be taking your chances and could well end up a few weeks later with a table full of brown leaves. Hopefully, this will be a pretty long-term commitment, so consider the following options.

First-time plant owners will probably want to start with a pre-assembled model. When you pick it out of a lineup, you can be pretty sure of what you're getting in size and shape and growing tendencies.

Those with some experience or a deeper nurturing instinct might prefer to start from scratch with seeds, bulbs, or cuttings. They certainly take more time and effort, and you might be in for some surprises (a darling little brown bulb that turns into a three-foot amaryllis, for example), but the satisfaction can be worth it all.

Caring For Adults

It's cute, the leaves are pretty, and it will go well with your leather sectional—if only it were so easy. There are, however, a few other considerations. Light, for example, and humidity. Put your Pollyanna notions of plant sellers aside—for some reason they'll stock plants that look cuddly and exotic but are best grown on Tibetan mountaintops. Plop them in the corner of an urban two-bedroom apartment and they'll act like E.T. in captivity.

Make sure you find out exactly what you're getting. There are suggestions in the following chapters but it's a drastically edited list. If you choose an unfamiliar plant, ask about its requirements—light, water, temperature, and humidity. Many have a little tongue depressor–like thing stuck in the soil with most of that information. Keep in mind that, like an ASPCA puppy, any plant you pick up is a work in progress. It will grow—fill out or up, depending on how you take care of it.

Before You Adopt

In plant adoption, there are several schools of thought. One is that you should just go to the nursery, fall in love, and deal with the consequences later—a sort of Vegas marriage. More sensible, and probably more enduring, is the school of careful deliberation, whereby you consider all the options and qualifications of both your home and the plant. Do you want something to go on the windowsill? Then a tree is not a good idea. Likewise, ivy is not the best choice for that spot on the floor behind the big armchair. Take the scale into account: how big it is, the shape of its leaves, its rate of growth.

What to Look for

Chances are, you'll be faced with a selection of siblings, each in somewhat different shape. First, check the tops and bottoms of leaves. Look for holes, stickiness, or brown spots, which could be a sign of pests; look as well for the pests themselves.

Pick it up and check the bottom of the pot. If the roots are all tangled up, the plant is probably root-bound, and the roots are strangling the plant. Try to ignore your humanitarian instincts and pick one with a healthier root structure.

If it's a flowering plant and beginning to bloom, pick out one with a lot of buds that are not yet fully opened. Those that are already in full bloom may be pretty to look at right now, but they're further along in the life cycle and will be more quick to fade.

TIP: Under Quarantine

If you've got other plants at home, it's a good idea to keep new arrivals separate for a few weeks. Pests are not always easy to spot and could be hiding, waiting for the right moment to migrate to the neighbors. Check the new arrival every day—under the leaves and around the stem—putting it with the others only when you're confident it's disease-free.

Relocation

Unless you want to display that brown or green plastic pot in the corner of your living room, you're going to want to repot your new acquisition. You could just stick the plastic pot inside another, more attractive container, but ultimately the plant will be better off with a fresh start.

The pot you choose should be about the same size or slightly larger than the plant's current home. If it's too small, it will become root-bound quickly; if you transplant it into an enormous pot, the plant will spend all of its energy trying to fill up its new home, and the part above the dirt line will suffer.

Starting from Scratch

On the pro side, there's a great ego boost that comes from putting a minute seed, a grungy-looking bulb, or a leaf in the ground and watching it turn into a plant. Plus, unless you're picking up some exotic Dutch tulip, it's a fraction of the cost. The cons are that patience is a requirement and success is far from guaranteed. In fact the whole process can be incredibly frustrating, since it's not uncommon to put months into the care and feeding of a newborn only to have the ungrateful creature whither up and die on you. Don't get depressed—these things happen to even the most seasoned gardeners (though they'd never admit it). Learn from your mistakes—perhaps there was not enough light or you overwatered. If you're up for experimenting, try planting the same seeds in different conditions and see how they react.

Bulbs

For the beginning gardener, bulbs are a good bet because most are pretty easy to grow and the results can be spectacular. Basically, a bulb is an entire flower structure jam-packed inside a pear-shaped container (corms and tubers are similar to bulbs except in shape and a bunch of other technical ways not worth mentioning).

Most can be planted in either soil or water. If you opt for the former, fill a container with dampened soil, then dig out a hole and stick the bulb in so that the thick round end faces down. The top, which is where the stem will pop out, should stick out above soil level. If you are growing more than one in a pot, group them closely together.

Planting in water provides you with one of those home nature experiences, whereby you get to watch the roots spread out from the bottom of the bulb. Special bulb containers, which are constructed with a water reservoir that narrows to form a sort of shelf where the bulb rests and sends its roots into the water below, are available at most plant stores. Another, slightly more primitive option is to fill the bottom of a glass container, such as a vase, with small rocks and fill it with water to just below the top of the rocks. Balance the bulb on the rocks and watch it sprout.

You can buy bulbs through catalogs or garden stores. Different varieties are "programmed" to sprout at different times of the year and only after certain conditions are met. Meeting all those conditions on your own—called forcing a bulb—is a pain in the butt involving refrigeration and paper bags so it's best to buy them ready to plant. When you shop, look for firm bulbs free of bruises and dents.

Depending on the effect you want to achieve, you can either plant them singly or bunch them together in a large pot. Some of the tall sprouters, like the amaryllis, might need a little support once their stems get lanky. Insert a long stick, or even a couple of chopsticks glued together, into the dirt next to it, and tie it to the stem. Like any other plant, it's going to reach toward the sun so an occasional pot rotation will also help it stay vertical.

Some good bulbs to try are:

Amaryllis: Huge and very impressive, one bulb can produce as many as four trumpet-shaped flowers. Depending on how the bulb was conditioned, you can find them ready to shoot up with

Repotting Made Easy

1. About an hour before the operation, water the plant you're going to move. This will make it easier to remove from the pot. Also, if you're going to use any sort of porous pot, like clay, soak it thoroughly so it won't hoard all the moisture, leaving its new occupant dry.

2. Get everything ready so you won't be running around with filthy fingers trying to find that darn pot. Spread newspaper across the area where you'll be working and lay everything out on top of it: The plant in its container, the new home, dirt, and a scissors or a knife in case you need to do some root trimming.

3. Most plant experts recommend leaving the hole in the bottom of the pot unplugged. However, if the hole is on the large side and you don't want dirt to escape through it, then cut a piece of screen just big enough to cover the hole and lay it out on the bottom of the pot.

4. Using a scooper or your hands, fill the bottom of the pot with fresh, moist soil. Don't put in too much dirt, or you won't leave enough room for the plant and its roots. About a quarter of an inch of new soil should do it.

5. Gently tip the plant upside down into your hand—your palm flat against the soil, fingers on either side of the stem—and bang on the bottom of the pot to loosen it from the roots. Don't pull at the stem or you might decapitate the plant. If you're having trouble getting it out, scrape around the sides with a dull kitchen knife or other flat object.

6. Once you've got the plant out of the container, use your thumbs to push up into the dirt and loosen the root structure, or root ball. You might break some roots, which is okay. The purpose of this is to encour-

oops

age them to spread out. The all-too-common result of ignoring this step is a sad and mildly embarrassing problem called alienated plant syndrome, when two years after you've lovingly repotted your plant, you realize that the roots remained tangled up in their original shape and never took advantage of the new space to expand. This is also the time to check for pests, like mealybugs, or rotted roots, which can be cut out with scissors or a pruner. Pick out any pebbles or other clingy foreign matter from the roots.

7. Put the plant into the pot, adding more dirt below if necessary to adjust its position. In smaller pots, leave from half an inch to an inch between the top of the plant's root structure and the rim of the container. In larger pots, you should leave up to two inches to allow room for watering. Fill the rest of the pot with dirt, making sure the sides are well packed, though not so cramped as to prevent circulation and damage the roots. After you've filled it, tap the pot on a hard surface so the dirt settles into any air pockets.

8. Water thoroughly, focusing on the edges of the pot, until it begins to run out of the drainage hole (make sure you dump the water out of the saucer or you might begin the process of death by drowning).

orange, red, pink, or white flowers for the winter holidays or in the springtime. Amaryllises prefer lots of sun and moist soil, and can grow up to eighteen inches high.

Crocus: You'll probably see preplanted crocuses for sale in midwinter, which will lead to a late-winter/early spring show of cup-shaped flowers on a five-inch stalk. The Dutch hybrids tend to produce the best results, with flowers in mauve, white, purple, yellow, or a combination of colors. Cool, filtered sun and damp soil are the only requirements; no fertilizing is necessary. Unfortunately, crocuses tend to bloom only once—you can try to nurture them through a year of dormancy but prepare for disappointment.

Dahlia: They come in a variety of colors—yellow, lavender, red, and pink—and naturally shoot up in the summer or early fall. Nurseries produce specially stunted dwarf dahlias for containers, which will grow to anywhere from one to two feet. Immediately after planting, put the container in a cool, shady spot until the shoots appear, then move it to a sunny location. Don't overwater, and when you do add moisture avoid getting the foliage wet because it can become mildewed.

Hyacinth: Another springtime bloomer, hyacinths are most often seen in white, pink, or blue and look sort of like colorful fluffy pinecones. They will grow to about six inches and look best when grouped together in a pot or, if single, grown in a glass container. For best results, give them filtered sun and keep the soil moist. Whether they'll bloom again the following year is a bit of a crapshoot. Some will, others just lie dormant.

Lily of the valley: You've probably seen the white version of these stalks with tiny, bell-shaped flowers, but they are also available in red and yellow. They're best planted in soil, and within a month, will grow about three feet tall and send out sweet-smelling flowers that last several weeks. Keep them in a sunny window and beware of the berries they produce, which are poisonous—so clip them off if you have pets. These flowers naturally bloom in the spring, but you can buy them ready for a winter display.

Paper whites: These practically foolproof bulbs are a surefire sign of the winter holidays. Delicate white flowers appear at the ends of stems that grow about fifteen inches long, making an especially elegant display when grouped together. They do well in most conditions, but prefer low light. Enjoy them while they last, because paper whites can't be forced a second time.

Tulips: Though you tend to think of them in outdoor gardens, some varieties of tulips make the trip indoors, most of those blooming in the winter. You could pick up regular bulbs and try to force them, but why not let the nursery do the work for you? Buy some that are already forced and ready to go and plant them in a soil-filled container. Tulips don't do well in the heat—anything above 65°F or so will cause them to fade and whither—so put them in a cool place, such as a windowsill. Some bulbs can be recycled for the following year; unfortunately tulips are not one of them. After they're gone, say good-bye.

Feeling Cocky?

Let's say your bulbs grew up without a hitch and you became attached to the little guys. Storing them and conditioning them for the next year is a bit of a gamble, but it doesn't hurt to try. Though there's a different procedure for each type of bulb, the generalities tend to be the same. Some, like tulips and hyacinths, are very difficult to bring back. Amaryllis and lily of the valley are worth attempting.

After the flower has bloomed and died, pinch it off, leaving the stems attached. Over the next few weeks the bulb will suck that energy back from the stems, so keep feeding and watering, but gradually taper off as the stem begins to wither up and turn yellow. When the leaves are completely yellowed and wilted, pull them out and stop watering the bulb. You can either leave it in the pot or gently remove it and wrap it up in a paper bag. This is the bulb's extended nap-time; it needs approximately six weeks to regain its strength and during that time should be kept in a cool, dark place like the back of a closet.

After the six weeks are up (there's no alarm clock here, it can be longer if you forget), it needs a cold spell so put it in the refrigerator for three weeks. Take it out and treat it like a new bulb.

Making Babies

Cuttings are a brilliant and fairly simple way to steal your friends' plants at no cost to you beyond the soil and the pot. All it takes is one leaf or stem, depending on what type of plant you're raiding. Most, but not all plants are suitable for cuttings, and the results are far from guaranteed so don't get too discouraged if the offspring turn brown.

Some plants will do just about everything short of planting their progeny themselves. Spider plants and aloe, for example, grow little offshoots complete with roots; all you have to do is clip them off and stick them in dirt. Others, such as ivy, can be reproduced in a few different ways. Sometimes it will be obvious just by looking at the plant; if not, experiment—you've got nothing to lose but a branch or two.

There are a few rules of thumb for determining which plants work best with which procreation methods, but keep in mind they're by no means iron-clad. If it has long stems with staggered leaves in between, like philodendron or ivy, you're probably going to want to take a branch cutting. Plants with long leaves, like mother-in-law's tongue, and those with prominent veins in the leaves, like many begonias, usually reproduce best by cutting part or all of a leaf.

Steal your friends' plants—all it takes is one leaf or stem.

Cuttings

The most common reproduction method is to grow a new plant from a branch or leaf segment. To make a branch cutting, pick out a stem and count down a few leaves. Use a sharp knife or pruners and make a clean cut just below the node (the point where a leaf grows out of the stem) of the leaf farthest from the end; cut off that bottom leaf as well. Place the newly stripped end in a glass of water so that the leaves are above the water-line. Within a few weeks, you should see roots growing from the stem.

Fill a pot with soil or rooting mixture. An even better option is sphagnum moss (available at most garden supply shops and many hardware stores), which holds water well and is light enough to allow roots to breathe. Using the end of a pencil, make holes in the mix and plant the stem or stems, since you can plant several stems in one pot. Water regularly until you see new growth, at which point you'll know you've created a new plant. Give it some time to develop, then repot it in a new home.

TIP: Concocting Your Own Soil

For most of your purposes, a regular soil mix is sufficient, but to give an extra edge to seeds and cuttings, you might want to whip up a lighter potting mix. One pretty standard one includes one third regular potting soil, one third vermiculite or perlite (those little white things that lighten the soil and help it hold water longer), and one third peat moss.

TIP: Propagation Insurance

You can up the odds of success, especially with more difficult species, by using sphagnum moss instead of soil. It's airy enough to allow the cutting to produce roots easily and it holds water well so you won't have to be quite as diligent in watching over the newborn. Fill a small pot with sphagnum moss, poke a stem-size hole in the center, and stick in the cutting. Sphagnum moss does not have a whole lot of nutrient value, however, so as soon as you see new growth, move the plant to regular soil.

Other plants, often those with thick leaves, can grow roots straight from a dismembered leaf. The wandering Jew and the corn plant both reproduce best this way. All you do is remove a healthy leaf, stick it in soil, and wait for it to work its own magic.

Layering

In sort of a horticultural contortionist act with a twist, some leggier species can grow roots straight from the still-attached stem, which is basically why there's so much ivy in the world. All you do is align another pot of soil next to your plant, lay a stem across the soil (or better yet, rooting mixture) of the new pot and wait until it develops roots. When it does, snip it off and transfer it to a new home.

Air Layering

You've probably come across someone with one of those tall, woody plants that have lost all their lower leaves and look somewhat like Lurch from the Addam's Family—all stringy stem and full-head. That plant is not about to replenish itself from below, so the best solution is to propagate through air layering and send the original to horticultural heaven. To do this, stick a stake in the soil and attach it to the stem. Cut a slit right below where the foliage begins, brush rooting hormone (available at plant stores) over the wound, stuff some moss in the slit and wrap the whole area in more moss. Tie plastic around the top and bottom of the moss to hold it in place. Roots should eventually form and become visible through the plastic covering. At this point, cut through the stem just below the roots and pot the new plant.

Division

If it grows in a clump, it can probably be split up into separate plants. As much as people complain about how difficult it is to grow African violets, they're incredibly easy to split up, offering you double the chance of success (or failure—but stick with the optimistic view). Using your fingers or, if it's more stubborn, a knife, separate out a small clump, one which includes a cluster of leaves and developed roots. Stick it in soil, water, and hope for the best.

Use your fingers, or if it's more stubborn, a knife.

Seeds

By far the most uncertain, yet also most rewarding start-from-scratch option, growing from seed is pretty much restricted to those with decent light or an artificial light setup. Some seeds are easier to grow than others but all require more care and attention than a mature plant. In general, the best time to start them is in the spring, when the sunlight increases in length and intensity. However, read the directions on the seed package to find out the planting specifics, such as whether you need to soak seeds in water first (this speeds up germination), when, and how deep to plant them. Most quality seeds will be good for two seasons or even more, so store unused seeds in a dry, cool place—an airtight jar makes a good insulator.

Keep in mind that not all seeds are going to work in containers. Some, especially those that grow fat and tall, need more root space than a container can deliver. If you're not sure, ask at the nursery.

TIP: Best Bets

Like plants, some seeds are more foolproof than others. A few more likely to feed your eco-ego are:

- Aster
- Basil
- Catnip
- Cosmos
- Four-o'clock
- Marigold
- Nasturtium
- Nicotiana

TIP: The Three-Foot Stem

The moment that little shoot pops out of the soil is so gratifying that you don't want to admit something has gone awry when it stretches out to some awkward length and collapses without developing any leaves other than those two top propeller wings. Most likely, this is caused by insufficient light. Move it to a brighter spot and, after the first set of real leaves develop, transplant it, burying the stem up to where the leaves start under the dirt (if the stem is especially long, you can plant it at an angle).

Where to Begin

1. You can start seeds in almost any small vessel—paper cups, plastic deli containers, and egg cartons are great for multiple seeds. Either line the bottom of the container with pebbles for drainage or poke out some drainage holes, and fill about three quarters of the container with dampened soil or a seed mix.

2. Plant the seeds according to the package directions. The general practice is to plant at a depth about twice the length of the seed. Don't cluster them too closely or they'll have to fight for space and what you'll see is a show of Darwinism and disappointing results. A good rule of thumb is to leave a space of one inch between smaller seeds, and two inches between the larger ones. Teeny tiny seeds like strawberries and tomatoes can stay closer to the surface; buried too deep, they'll just get lost and never find the energy to push out stems. Larger seeds, like nasturtium and marigold, prefer a little more depth.

3. Spritz with water—not too much or the buried seeds will float to the top. A mister bottle is a handy way to wet down the soil without dousing it.

4. Forget every rule you ever learned about oxygen and wrap the container in a plastic bag, using a piece of string or a twist tie to secure it. This will trap moisture and provide the humidity that the seed needs to germinate. At this juncture, light is not a big consideration and you can leave the container in a shady area.

5. When you see a shoot, get excited but not too excited. The two little leaves at the end are what feed the roots and are pretty much the same on every newborn. Take it out of the plastic and water sparingly. This is the time it needs a healthy dose of light, warm temperatures, and enough water to keep it moist, but not soaked.

6. The next leaves are the real ones. After they appear, you can transplant the seedling to its new home. To do that, scoop out carefully (under the roots if possible) with a spoon or similar tool and transfer into a pot of soil. Add water. If you've damaged the roots, the plant might droop for a few days. Don't panic. As long as the damage is limited, it will recover.

Newborns

Another option is to let someone else do the preliminary work and pick them up as seedlings. These are generally sold in flats, or plastic containers divided up into rows of little square compartments, with one seedling to a compartment. Depending on where you look, you can find anything from tomatoes, peppers, and herbs, to flowers from alyssum to zinnia. Many, especially the flowers, are annuals and will be found at nurseries in the spring and summer. Seedlings can be repotted into pots or window boxes and generally look best grouped together en masse.

Making Your Pick

When you're shopping for seedlings, you'll probably come across a big, mildly overwhelming area of flats. Once you've decided which type of plant you're looking for, make sure to pick out the healthiest specimens. Look for seedlings with plenty of green, hearty-looking leaves. Avoid those that are droopy, or look like they're fighting for space. For the flowering seedlings, keep an eye out for those with a lot of unopened buds.

The Big Move

Transplant seedlings the same way you would plants. Partially fill a container with moistened soil. Using a wide dull knife, spoon, or similar utensil, dig deep into the soil, getting underneath the seedling's root structure. Carefully transfer the whole clump into the waiting container. For the first few weeks, don't fertilize; keep it moist until it starts growing, then treat as you would any other plant.

To encourage full development, pinch off any leggy growth. If you want to encourage more flowers, pinch off any buds and existing flowers as well.

If you're going to be grouping a lot of seedlings together, just lay them out on top of the soil together and rearrange until you're satisfied with how they look. Then you can fill the rest of the container and water until the excess runs out of the bottom of the

Be sure to pick the healthiest specimens.

pot. Don't hesitate to experiment and group a number of different species together in one container. As long as there's plenty of space down below the existing roots, you shouldn't have to worry about them crowding each other.

TIP: Fertilizing Guidelines

The same way you wouldn't go feeding four-alarm chili to an infant, sprouting seeds, cuttings, and freshly planted seedlings need a carefully supervised diet of light and water. In other words, lay off the fertilizer until they've put down solid roots in their own homes.

Where to Go

You'll find plants for sale anywhere, from the grocery store to the farmer's market. There's no hard and fast rule that one source is better than another, but for the healthiest plants, you're better off shopping at a place that doesn't store them wedged between the detergent and the kitty litter.

Check out any prospective adoptees carefully and try to resist the urge to become a noble Charlie Brown by picking out the most wilted and sad-looking specimen in the hope that you can be its savior. It's a nice thought, but most likely you'll soon end up with a wilted dead plant and a case of mild depression. Check under the leaves and up and down the stems for bugs, examine the root structure as closely as possible, and look for dead or dying areas, possible signs of disease.

Seeds have a shelf life. Older ones are less likely to produce results, so if you're starting from scratch your best bet is to shop at a place with high turnover, or even better, one that marks packages with expiration dates. Catalogs are a good bet for seeds, as are nurseries.

If you order from a catalog, try not to get so carried away with the description that you end up with something that requires a five-foot root base. Let the customer service person know that you're horticulturally illiterate and spell out the exact conditions of your home. The following catalogs have customer hotlines manned by extremely plant-smart people:

Burpee Gardens
(800) 888-1447
The king of catalogs, Burpee has everything from miniature pumpkins to imported marigolds.

The Gourmet Gardener
(913) 345-0490
It lists mostly fruit and vegetable seeds, many of which can be grown in containers. Plus there's a container gardening section, with herbs and edible flowers.

Shepherd's Garden Seeds
(860) 482-3638
Great for beginners, Shepherd's includes seed starter kits and the catalog itself has tips on growing and troubleshooting.

Thompson & Morgan
(800) 274-7333
This splashy slick catalog also has a section on containers. Their phone service is incredibly helpful, and they'll help you to pick out the best seeds and seedlings for your environment.

Replanting

There comes a time in most plants' lives when they must move out of their starter homes and into a bigger space. Sometimes, you'll know right off the bat—the roots grow out of the drainage

*There comes a time in most plants' lives when they must move out
of their starter homes and into a bigger space.*

holes or sides of the pot, or the container is lost in a morass of branches and leaves. More likely, the plant will just get droopy and you won't necessarily know what's wrong. If the latter is the case, gently remove the plant from its container and check the roots. The plant is root-bound if they are in a tangled mess with no room for expansion. If so, it's time to repot and you should follow the directions on pages 28–29 under "Repotting Made Easy," transplanting it to a pot one or two sizes larger than its current home. If you want to be really conscientious, a good rule of thumb is to repot your plants once a year; if you do them all at the same time you get the work and the mess over with all at once.

Maintenance for the Oversized

If you get a backache just thinking about repotting your five-foot tree, there are a couple of other solutions. Topdressing once a year or so will keep the plant healthy for a few extra years by giving it a dose of fresh nutrients. Scrape off as much of the soil at the top of the pot as you can without exposing major roots. Then refill with fresh soil and fertilize.

Topdressing won't stop your tree from getting root-bound and saggy at some point in the future. If you want to revive it, you can perform a drastic root-pruning operation. Get someone to help you remove the plant from its pot. Using a sharp knife, cut away approximately four to six inches at the sides and base of the root ball, then repot it in its old home using fresh dirt. This is also good for smaller plants you would prefer to keep on the diminutive side. The plant might go into shock and look incredibly depressed for a few weeks, but have patience and it will come back to life.

chapter three

Plants
for
Beginners

Building Confidence

The secret to ego-boosting gardening is to start with assured success and slowly graduate to the bigger challenges. Most of the plants in this chapter thrive with relatively little attention, so no matter how neglectful you are, they'll endure. And the beauty is that no one else will realize you're a novice. All have great-looking greenery and expansive personalities.

Indestructibles

Short of silk or plastic, you'd be hard-pressed to find a plant more difficult to slay than one of these.

Ivy

The blue blood of plants, ivy is versatile, fast growing, and impressive looking. The same properties that make it a brick-wall favorite on the university campus also make it a standout houseplant. You can let it trail over the windowsill or train it to climb a trellis, a lamp, or anything else it can grab hold of with its long clingy stems. There are a number of different species, some of the most popular being grape, English, and Swedish, any of which will grow until it runs out of room.

Light: Most ivies need a good two to three hours of direct sunlight a day in order to maintain their two-tone color but can make do with bright, indirect light.

Sustenance: Ivies need a fair amount of water, but wait until the top half-inch or so dries out before adding more.

Reproduction: Another of ivy's great attributes is that it's so easy to make more ivy. Stick the stems of cuttings into a glass of water and leave them alone until they develop roots. Or, as previously mentioned, try layering—align another pot of soil next to the plant's current domicile and place a couple of stems

Train it to climb a trellis, a lamp, or anything else it can grab hold of.

across the new pot. Within a few weeks, roots should form; clip and plant them in their new home.

Troubleshooting: If it starts to grow straggly with long gaps between leaves, cut it back to induce it to fill out. Browning ivy is probably getting too much water or its roots are strangling the plant.

The Down and Dirty: Ivy is a pro at covering all those wall imperfections. Let it droop over the water spots under the windowsill; to hide scuff marks or holes left by the wall-hanging you decided you couldn't stand, prop a trellis against the area you want to conceal and let the ivy go wild.

TIP: The Highs and Lows

Ivy may be the chameleon of plants, taking on whatever shape seems appropriate for the growing conditions, but there are other types of climbers and trailers that are also relatively easy to train and maintain.

If you've got your heart set on a trailing plant, here are a few that either work great on their own or as a dangling frame for one or more contained species:

- Wandering Jew or its cousin the chain plant.
- Creeping fig or ficus, which is related to the more upstanding weeping fig.
- Creeping Charlie, which has yellowish rounded leaves and is incredibly easy to keep healthy with low light and damp soil.

If you want a climber to train up a trellis or stake, here are two low-maintenance options:

- Velvet plant, which has burgundy leaves and tiny purple hairs that grab on to the support system.
- Kangaroo vine, which has glossy leaves and thrives in cooler conditions.

Finer foliaged climbers, like leadwort, look great trained to follow a gentle arc, like the handle of a basket or a looped stick.

Aloe

You can save a fortune on the drugstore potions by growing your own. They aren't as elegant as some other plants, but if you're looking for function and durability in one spiky package that can grow up to three feet high, this is it.

Light: Aloe can tolerate anything from bright indirect to direct sunlight, but will not do well without at least a few hours of brightness.

Sustenance: Despite its cactuslike appearance, the aloe prefers moist soil.

Reproduction: Not one for subtle reproduction, the aloe presents its babies up front, producing offshoots from its stems that can be directly planted in soil and distributed to all your friends.

Troubleshooting: If the entire plant tips over, don't panic. They do this naturally. Since it's a pretty hardy plant, few things will make it sick. If it does appear to be coming down with something, it's probably due to a lack of light or water.

The Down and Dirty: It's a great plant for klutzes who tend to burn or cut themselves often since the sap of the plant is very soothing. Simply break off a leaf and split it open to extract the aloe vera.

Philodendron

This is the classic beginner's plant. The most common variety is the heart-leaved philodendron, which has bright green foliage, thick leathery leaves, grows like a weed unless you trim it back, and can easily be brought back from the deathbed when you forget to water it.

Light: Keep it out of direct sunlight, which will burn the leaves. Though it does okay in low light, the stems may get long and stringy and you'll have to pinch it back so it doesn't look like the gangly supermodel of houseplants. Bright indirect light is the best option.

Sustenance: If you're an incredibly forgetful person, this is the plant for you. It doesn't need a whole lot of water and when it gets severely dehydrated it will flatten out like a squashed bug. Reviving it is actually a fascinating experience—once you soak the soil, the plant will perk up in minutes, making you feel omnipotent.

Reproduction: This is the plant to give to every friend, relative, and co-worker because it's so easy to churn out a whole family from one parent. Just take your cuttings and stick the ends of the stems into a pot.

Troubleshooting: The philodendron tends to get all stretched out and scraggly looking so it could use fairly frequent pinching. Clip off the leggy stems just past a leaf node to make the growth bushier.

The Down and Dirty: Like ivy, the philodendron can be trained to grow upward or allowed to dangle down over a windowsill or countertop. It makes a great office plant, showing off your great nurturing instincts while hiding the coffee spots on your desk. The easiest way to make it climb is to give it something wet and clingy to grip—it loves moss-covered stakes. Train the plant by tying or stapling the stems to the stake; after initial contact it will climb on its own.

TIP: To Prune or Not to Prune

A lot of plants need to be reined in once in a while or they begin to look more like straggly weeds than healthy plants. However, there are species that actually look better all stretched out and skinny. Hanging plants, for example, can look okay with slender tendrils hanging down, and some people like their philodendrons long and lanky.

Jade Plant

For more fastidious types who can't abide leaf shedding or leggy extensions, the jade plant is an ideal corner decoration. It has thick shiny leaves, edged in red on some plants. They can grow up to four feet tall, but they'll take their sweet time doing it.

Light: A few hours of direct sunlight is the best situation for jade plants. They can do pretty well with bright indirect light as well, though the growth won't be as lush.

Sustenance: Their thick leaves act as a sort of water reservoir, so jade plants need less frequent watering than most other plants. Allow the soil to get pretty dry between watering and when you do nourish it, wet the soil thoroughly.

Reproduction: Take stem cuttings about three inches long and plant them directly in a container. To survive, jade babies need bright light and a generous amount of water. They take a pretty long time to root—often several months—so be patient.

Troubleshooting: If you prefer a diminutive plant, keep it in a small container. Otherwise, give it room to grow by repotting it about once a year. Don't go more than an inch or so larger at a time, however, or it will get overwhelmed and depressed.

The Down and Dirty: With a jade plant, you pretty much know what you're getting and unless you go for growth, you can force it to look the same for years—all of which makes it a great option for controlling types and the hyper-neat.

Spider Plant

With its spindly offshoots, often up to three feet long, the spider plant is a great decorative piece. The leaves are green with yellow stripes down the center and it presents its own miniature offshoots, which often show up in groups between the parent leaves.

Light: Some direct sunlight is not a bad idea, but spider plants will do fine in bright indirect light. A lack of sufficient brightness may cause the leaves to lose their dual color distinction.

Sustenance: These are thirsty plants and need a fair amount of water to thrive. Keep the soil moist without allowing it to sit in a puddle of water.

Reproduction: Talk about your cooperative plants. The spider plant presents its babies, generally in the spring, in the form of tiny plants. When the leaves on these offshoots are about three inches long, simply snip the whole thing off and transfer it into its own pot.

Troubleshooting: If the leaf tips get brown, it's either getting too much midday intense sunlight—move it to a location with late or early sun or just a bright place with no direct light—or it's not getting enough water. If the roots have grown out of the top of the pot and are making it difficult to water the plant, it's time to move your spider plant to a new, roomier home.

The Down and Dirty: This can be a very impressive-looking plant, so show it off. Plant it on a pedestal so the arch of the leaves looks most impressive. Of the easy plants, this probably needs the most attention, however, so it's not for the frequent traveler or the incredibly forgetful.

It's not for the frequent traveler or the incredibly forgetful.

Wandering Jew

Though its life span is relatively short (about three to four years), this plant is worth adopting for its brilliant color display. The leaves have a striated green top and bright purple undersides and grow up to several feet in a sort of controlled haphazard way—pointing in various directions—off their trailing stems.

Light: Like most plants with colored leaves, the wandering Jew needs bright light and does best with a couple of hours of direct sunlight a day.

Sustenance: Keep the soil thoroughly moist without letting it get too soggy.

Reproduction: Since the mother plant will fizzle out in a few years, the best way to keep her spirit alive is through her off-spring. Take cuttings of the brightly colored leaves (the paler ones are less likely to set roots) about three inches long. Insert several of them in a soil-filled pot and place it in a bright spot. Water just enough to keep the soil moist. The roots should develop in about two weeks.

Troubleshooting: If the leaves start to look dull or the stems get straggly, the plant is probably not getting enough light. For all its beauty, this plant tends to have a fair amount of sickly look-ing growth as well. Don't be afraid to cut it away. Eventually the whole plant will begin to look sad and dull. Give it a proper burial and put a cutting in its place.

The Down and Dirty: Another great decorator-type plant, the wandering Jew is very impressive as a centerpiece. Try it in a colored pot—green, for example—with an aged finish to set off the colors.

Cast-Jron Plant

With a name like that, you know you've got a low-maintenance species. The leaves are about fifteen inches long and two inches wide and they grow straight out of the pot, one big, glossy leaf per stem.

Light: Though you could put it pretty much anywhere and it would survive, the cast-iron plant does best in medium light, such as a sun-free window.

Sustenance: Allow the soil to get dry between waterings, as one of the few things that can kill the cast-iron plant is too much water.

Reproduction: Separate out two or more leaves from the rhizomes (the firm tubelike source of the leaf located below the soil), attempting to include some of the plant's roots with the package. Plant them in a small pot and water sparingly until you see new growth.

Troubleshooting: Brown-spotted leaves are a sign of overwatering, and eventually the plant will turn completely brown and wither away. Scorched leaf tips could indicate light that's too intense.

The Down and Dirty: Since they're relatively simple looking, one of the best ways to get a dramatic effect from a cast-iron plant is to group several plants together or use one as a centerpiece for an arrangement. If you prefer to keep it simple, try using a more decorative container, such as an etched terra-cotta pot or, if you're feeling more adventurous, an old jumbo soup or tomato can.

Northern Exposure

If you're under the mistaken impression that you need a bright sunny room to show off your plants, take a look in your local bank. Chances are, one of the following plants is thriving in some dark corner.

White Sails (Spathiphyllum)

Forgive the Latin, but there are so many names for this plant it's easy to confuse. It's a very common plant in low-light businesses like banks and lawyers' offices because the glossy leaves and white flowers create a distracting and somewhat soothing atmosphere while you're sitting in the dark getting audited. Each leaf grows straight from the soil to about fifteen inches in length before withering up to make room for its replacement.

Light: It can survive, even thrive, on the bare minimum.

Sustenance: Let the top inch of soil dry out before watering. When it's neglected, the white sails will collapse so dramatically that you'll be ready to bury it and bear the guilt trip, but with a good dousing of water it will spring back to life.

Reproduction: Separate a few leaves and their rhizomes, trying to include the roots. Replant in a small container.

Troubleshooting: For some reason, this plant tends to attract bugs, so check the leaves frequently. Scorched leaves probably indicate too much sun.

The Down and Dirty: It's a great decorative plant for the horticulturally uninitiated because it looks so elaborate. Plant it in a colorful container and use it to add life to a dark corner.

Rubber Plant

Living up to its moniker, the rubber plant has very thick large leaves that feel elastic to the touch. It's very simple—the leaves shoot directly off the center stem—and can take a fair amount of neglect without shriveling up. The rubber plant can grow up to two to three feet, with leaves as long as fifteen inches each.

Light: Keep it in low light—anywhere from a dark corner to a spot with indirect sun.

Sustenance: Overwatering can also be deadly to the rubber plant. Let it dry out in between doses.

Reproduction: Unfortunately, this is an extremely difficult plant to propagate. The process involves a lot of time and patience so you're better off buying a new one.

Troubleshooting: As simple as this plant is in its demands, it is pretty sensitive about getting too much of anything. Too much water will cause its leaves to fall off; direct sun will turn them brown. Its shiny leaves also attract dust which, while it won't kill them, will make you look like a bad housekeeper. Sponge them off with water occasionally.

The Down and Dirty: The rubber plant is a great choice for someone who travels a lot or forgets that water is a necessity. Its bulk looks best in a light-colored heavy-duty container, like a stone urn or a whitewashed clay pot.

Dumb Cane

Also called the mother-in-law's tongue (don't ask), the dumb cane has very large leaves that fan out in a sort of dramatic gesture.

They can grow as high as five feet, but tend to lose a lot of lower leaves in the process so they look best in a more diminutive state.

Light: They can tolerate anything from indirect sun to a shady spot in the corner.

Sustenance: Like most of its low-light cousins, the dumb cane can deal with infrequent watering, and actually does best when allowed to dry out a bit in between.

Reproduction: Though it can take a while to root, you can plant a stem that includes at least two leaves. Kept in indirect light, it should settle in within four to six weeks.

Troubleshooting: One suggested source of the name dumb cane is the poisonous nature of the plant's sap. If it comes in contact with the mouth it can cause swelling and loss of speech so wash your hands after touching it. When they age, they tend to lose their lower leaves. This is common and it's not your fault. To revive and return the plant to its initial splendor, try air layering (see Chapter 2, page 35).

The Down and Dirty: The smaller plants look best when placed in an elevated setting so you can see the gentle arch of the leaves. An older dumb cane can stand as a tree in the corner.

Prayer Plant

So-named for its pious tendency to fold leaf pairs together at night, the prayer plant has foliage in shades of green marked by raised red veins in a rib-cage pattern. Though the stems are generally allowed to drape over the container, they can be trained up a pole and, allowed plenty of root space, can grow several feet long.

Light: It can thrive anywhere without direct sun, but does best in a room with a fair amount of indirect light.

Sustenance: Prayer plants need frequent watering and the soil should be kept moist.

Reproduction: Take cuttings from a stem with at least three or four leaves and plant in a shady spot. The roots take about four to six weeks to form.

Troubleshooting: Too much light will cause the leaves to lose their color and turn brown at the edges. With a lack of water, the leaves will get droopy.

The Down and Dirty: This is a great plant to show off, especially with its folding leaf party trick. A simple container with fairly shallow sides is the best option so the leaves will become the centerpiece.

Swiss Cheese Plant

Distinctive slits in the leaves develop when this plant ages, adding distinction to its shiny light green foliage. In the wild, it grows up trees and other obstacles and, given ample root space, can be trained to do the same in captivity.

Light: While brighter indirect light provides the best growing conditions, this plant can do well in low light.

Sustenance: The Swiss cheese plant thrives on infrequent attention. Allow the soil to dry out before watering.

Reproduction: Because of the large leaves and their irregular growth pattern, this is a difficult plant to propagate. You're better off revisiting the plant store.

The Down and Dirty: The Swiss cheese plant is a great conversation piece and has a sort of haphazard growth pattern so play it up with a textured container, such as a ribbed terra-cotta pot or one with an interesting trim around the top.

Trees

For some reason, the bigger the plant, the more impressive it seems. Trees, for that reason, provide not only a great decorating tool to fill up barren corners, but to the untrained eye, they make you appear horticulturally invincible.

On the Smaller Side

Norfolk Island Pine

A slow-growing pine with delicate branches, the Norfolk Island pine grows very slowly, about six inches a year, and rarely gets larger than four feet when kept indoors.

Light: Although they won't be adversely affected by direct sun, this plant is best kept in medium light, with bright indirect sun.

Sustenance: More sensitive than some of the other trees mentioned here, this one needs fairly diligent watering. Keep the soil moist, though be careful not to let it sit in a puddle.

Reproduction: Unfortunately, the Norfolk Island pine is very difficult to propagate.

Troubleshooting: At times, the branches may look as if they're ready to collapse sideways, but don't fear, they will eventually strengthen and right themselves. If the needles start falling off, it's probably not getting enough light.

The Down and Dirty: With its bright green needles and fanned-out shape, the Norfolk Island pine makes a great, Charlie Brown–like holiday tree. Decorate it with paper ornaments and miniature lights and toast your environmental sensibilities with eggnog.

TIP: Keep It Down

The size of your tree depends, to a large extent, on you. If you want it to grow big and tall, repot it every year in a larger container. Fans of more diminutive species can keep their trees in the same container and just trim the roots every couple of years.

Yucca

This one has a sort of combination space age and desert island appearance, with clusters of large, sword-shaped leaves growing out of what look like thick sticks. The whole thing rarely grows larger than about four feet.

Light: It needs a lot of light, at least three hours a day of direct sunlight, in order to grow and produce healthy leaves.

Sustenance: Although it really prefers to be kept in moist soil, the yucca can tolerate a certain amount of neglect and will most likely come back after stretches of sporadic watering.

Reproduction: It's an iffy proposition, but you can try propagating the yucca by chopping off a whole offshoot, or bunch of leaves along with their stem. Stick it in soil and put it in a bright spot, if possible one with filtered sun. If it works, the roots should take in about six weeks.

Troubleshooting: Since they get so top-heavy, plant the yucca in a sturdy container—clay, for example—or you may find the plant on its side. Sickly or droopy yuccas may not be getting enough light.

The Down and Dirty: It's a conversation piece so show it off in a prominent position—in front of the living room window, for example. Since it is pretty hardy, it's a good plant for the forgetful.

Parlor Palm

After years of growth, the parlor palm probably won't surpass three feet, but with its stubby green trunk and gently arching leaves, it has treelike stature.

Light: When you think about the palm's natural habitats, it makes sense that it needs a fair amount of bright light or it will get straggly.

Sustenance: Unlike most people, the parlor palm adores humidity so unless you want to live in a steam room you're going to have to water it regularly, enough to keep the soil thoroughly moist. Occasionally give it a really good dousing, so that the water runs through the pot.

Reproduction: Forget about it.

Troubleshooting: In overly arid conditions, the tips of the leaves might turn brown. If this is the case mist the leaves frequently to provide more humidity.

The Down and Dirty: Because of its somewhat funky, Miami-like feel, the parlor palm looks great in colored containers, such as a whitewashed pot or an old barrel.

TIP: The Thirsty Container

To some extent, how often you water your plant will depend on the type of container it calls home. If it's in a pot that absorbs some of the flow, such as terra-cotta or wood, you're going to have to be more diligent about watering it than if it's in a plastic or plastic-lined home.

A Taste of the Great Outdoors

Corn Plant

Though it's officially listed with a maximum height of five feet, these palmlike plants can easily reach ceiling height. The name provides a pretty accurate description; it has wide, variegated leaves that fan out as if peeled from an enormous ear of corn.

Light: The best positioning for the corn plant is in bright light without direct sun, which can burn the leaves.

Sustenance: Although it would prefer to live in perpetually moist soil, the corn plant is one that can survive a certain amount of forgetfulness with only some droopy leaves, then spring back to life when it finally gets some water.

Reproduction: You can either make a leaf cutting, stripping one away and planting it in soil, or, if the plant becomes overgrown and you want to start over, cut the stalk into small pieces about three inches long, each containing a node. Either plant the stalk vertically in soil or lay it horizontally across a pot of soil and within four to six weeks you should notice new growth; eventually you will have a whole new tree.

Troubleshooting: With age, corn plants can lose their lower leaves and look gangly. At this point you may want to sacrifice it to a new generation (see above). If you're going for maximum growth, repot it in a container a few inches larger, preferably in the spring.

The Down and Dirty: Corn plants are the classic corner decor, best when the stalk is obscured and the foliage sticks out, from behind a couch or table for example.

Weeping Fig

This is an elegant and graceful tree with arching stems and dangling leaves. It tends to be a bit more difficult to grow than some of the other plants mentioned here, partly because it's so prone to infestation from various pests. But if you can keep it healthy, it will eventually grow to about six feet.

Light: It will tolerate a great range of lighting situations, from direct sun to a reasonably well-lit room.

Sustenance: Water fairly infrequently, allowing the soil to get dry between sessions, but when you do water, pour it on and thoroughly wet the soil.

Reproduction: It's very difficult to propagate. You're best off getting a new tree.

Troubleshooting: Pests are the most common downfall of the weeping fig (see Chapter 6 for symptoms and treatments). At the change of seasons, it is common for the tree to go into shock and lose some leaves. It will recoup its losses when it adjusts to the new conditions.

The Down and Dirty: It's a beautiful tree, and looks best standing on its own in a simple container, such as a tan clay pot. The other big plus is that it fits into most decorating schemes, adding a touch of elegance to early modern or faded antiques.

Ferns

Erase those seventies associations of modular furniture, lava lamps, and groovy potted ferns from your mind. There is a huge variety of fern shapes and sizes, most of which will not give your living room a flashback motif. Some are trailers; others will stop growing at about fifteen inches.

Erase those seventies associations of modular furniture, lava lamps, and groovy potted ferns from your mind.

The basic distinction between ferns and most other plants is that ferns do not produce flowers or seeds, but instead reproduce with spores (tiny growths generally found on the underside of leaves). The fronds, which in fern parlance means leaves, range from the delicate lacy growths of the asparagus fern to the much wider, rosette clusters of the bird's nest fern. Most are easy to grow and maintain.

Basic Domesticated Ferns

Fine Fronds	Thick Fronds
Emerald fern	Bird's nest fern
Boston fern	Hare's fern
Button fern	Staghorn fern

Light: Although they're tropical plants, ferns are generally low-growing and are protected from the sun by their taller neighbors. Keep them out of direct sunlight; they'll do well in most other conditions, as long as there's some brightness.

Sustenance: Since they tend to lose moisture through their leaves, most ferns need diligent and bountiful watering. Keep the soil moist and when you add water, do it until the water runs through the soil and collects in the bowl below.

Reproduction: The easiest way to make new ferns is to divide the rhizomes. Take the plant out of the pot and shake off the excess dirt. At the bottom of each stem you'll find a sort of tube-shaped growth—that's the rhizome. With a sharp knife, remove one and cut it into several pieces, making sure each has a few fronds growing from it. Plant each rhizome piece in a small container with moist soil, allowing the fronds to stick out above soil level. It should root and show new growth in four to five weeks.

Troubleshooting: Ferns are very susceptible to pests, so watch out for fading fronds, brown patches, or the bugs themselves. Be careful with pesticides, as some will kill ferns. Read the label first.

The Down and Dirty: If you want to go for the retro ferns, keep a sense of humor about it. You might want to plant it in an offbeat container (group a few in an old Monkee's lunchbox, for example).

Cacti

This is the classic species for the rampant plant killer, though some are easier to care for than others. Because they have no leaves and store water in their bodies, cacti generally need very little attention and can survive a lot of neglect. Though they're not generally considered a flowering breed, many cacti do produce beautiful and abundant flowers annually. Some cacti are easier to reproduce than others. Small, self-contained cacti, such as the bishop's cap, will probably get the last laugh from any attempted cutting. Those that grow offshoots, like most rose pincushions, make it easy. Simply slice off an offshoot and plant it immediately in soil. Treat it as an adult.

There are two basic types of cacti: desert cacti and jungle cacti. The desert variety usually have spines, and the jungle ones don't. The light and watering needs of each individual plant vary. Following is a small sampling of good cacti to try out.

Rat's Tail

If you were scared by Audrey II in *Little Shop of Horrors*, beware: this is a long-legged cactus with prickly stems that can reach up to three feet. It needs a lot of light and enough water to dampen the soil once a week or so. In the spring it puts out spectacular pink flowers.

Bishop's Cap

This is a small, spherical cactus no more than a few inches tall, divided into segments and covered with what looks like fine silver fur. After a few years, it will begin to flower at the top, sending out cheerful yellow blooms throughout the summer. It needs bright, direct sunlight, at least a few hours a day. Let the soil dry out between waterings.

Golden Barrel

So it's not a cuddly plant, but it's certainly not run-of-the-mill. With a diameter of about four inches and a height of about six, the golden barrel looks like a ridged green baseball with hundreds of yellow spikes. It thrives only in direct sunlight, and needs at least three to four hours. Like most cacti, it will rot if given too much water, so add only enough to keep the soil from blowing away. Its more popular cousin, the barrel cactus, looks somewhat similar, but its spikes are brown and, unlike the golden barrel, it produces white, trumpet-shaped flowers.

Rose Pincushion

It's similar in shape to the golden barrel, but the rose pincushion has yellow and brown spikes and it forms beautiful red flowers in a ring around the top of the body. Give it as much direct sunlight as you can and water it sparingly.

Christmas Cactus

Even non-cactus lovers will like this jungle variety. It is made up of flattened green leaflike segments that join together to comprise what look like stems. Around the end of the year, each produces a long fuchsia flower. Direct sunlight will kill this cactus, so you can keep it in a bright room, but preferably away from windows. It also needs more water than the desert cacti, enough to keep the soil moist.

'Tis the Season

Like the unavoidable fruitcake, there are some plants that make an appearance every year around the holidays. Most, like the Christmas Pepper (see Chapter 4), are quick in, quick out. Others, if nurtured, will stick around for another year.

Poinsettia

This is the plant with the red leaves, the one that blankets the country in December then disappears by February. That's because it's a winter-flowering plant (the red leaves are considered flowers), with leaves that fade after a few months. The poinsettia is very easy to care for, demanding only filtered light and minimal water when the leaves start to droop. If you've got the energy, you could try to nurture it through another year by following a relatively labor-intensive process, but it spends half that time as a two-inch stump so you might as well just pick up a new one the following year.

Christmas Trees

You could save the expense and hassle of picking up a new Christmas tree every year by just keeping your own container-bound tree in the corner and dressing it up for the holidays. Many varieties of fir, pine, and spruce are available in miniature versions, standing anywhere from one to six feet. Kept in a container, they tend to be more slow-growing and need at least a few hours of bright light a day and moist—though never soggy—soil.

chapter four

Beyond the Green

Color Commentary

Sometimes you want a little extra payback for all that diligent watering, pruning, and all-around caretaking. Greenery is great, but nothing says, "Way to go!" like a burst of bright flowers. There's really no reason to be intimidated—you don't need an advanced pruning degree to grow flowering plants.

The availability of plants you'll find at the local nursery usually depends on the time of year you're looking. Generally, the greenhouse will display whatever is flowering or about to. Keep in mind that many of these plants are annuals and will display their wares only once, while perennials can be coaxed back year after year.

TIP: The First Painful Pinch

When your plant starts to flower, pinch off the initial blooming buds just below a node. It will probably hurt you more than the plant, but you'll both be happier in the end. It sends a message down the stem to send up reinforcements and you'll end up with a bushier plant with many more flowers.

Easy Bloomers

These flowering plants are surprisingly easy to grow, no more difficult than your garden-variety greenery.

Begonia

There's a huge variety of begonias out there; some are pretty foolproof houseplants, others are on the more difficult side. Wax begonia, a perennial that can grow up to three feet tall, is one of the most common and most cooperative. Its flowers can be red,

Greenery is great, but nothing says "Way to go!"
like a burst of bright flowers.

pink, or white and the bonus is that they stay in bloom for most of the year. A couple of other options are the angelwing and fuchsia begonias, both of which produce little flower clusters, generally in pink or red.

Light: Most flowering begonias will do best in bright light with a few hours of direct sunlight a day.

Sustenance: Overwatering is the bane of begonias. They need moderate moisture—allow the top of the soil to dry out before watering.

Reproduction: Most begonias are very easy to propagate. Take leaf or stem cuttings a few inches long and plant them directly into soil. Keep out of direct sun until they root, which should be in about three weeks.

Troubleshooting: For some reason, begonias are particularly susceptible to mildew, which shows up as powdery deposits on the leaves. Rinse leaves periodically with water and if you do fall prey to an attack, spritz the leaves with an antifungal plant soap.

The Down and Dirty: Since begonias—especially the wax begonia—can grow a pretty offbeat selection of leaves, try an equally eye-catching container if you're feeling bold, like your high school sports trophy (as long as you don't mind drilling the drainage holes).

Geranium

It's the classic flowering perennial, easy to grow, some with huge flowers in red, yellow, or pink; others with white or multicolored leaves. Most geraniums grow up to two feet. Some have scented leaves, though these types are grown mostly for their fragrance and few actually flower.

Light: Geraniums love the sun, the more rays the better. This is one reason they are often seen in window boxes.

Sustenance: Thanks to their thick stems and leaves, geraniums hold water well so they can feed themselves for a few days between waterings. As a general rule, you should wait until the top few inches of soil become dry before watering.

Reproduction: Because of their hardy nature, geraniums are good candidates for propagation. Take three-inch cuttings from new shoots, beginning directly below a node, or cut off any flowering buds and plant directly in a container.

Troubleshooting: As beautiful as blooming geranium flowers can be, they're pretty ugly when they're dead. Pinch back immediately, as this will also encourage the development of new shoots. Geraniums are also susceptible to black stem rot, which will quickly eat away and kill the entire plant. This is caused by too much moisture, either in the air or the soil so avoid overwatering.

The Down and Dirty: It's one of the easiest flowering plants to care for, so it's a good bet for that first foray into blooms. Though officially they flower from spring to fall, under the right conditions and a lot of luck, they can continue on year-round.

Amethyst Violet

As their name implies, these flowers are a bright purple surrounded by ribbed oval leaves. Considered annuals, they generally flower in the fall, and the blooms will last several weeks. It's unlikely they'll flower again after one season, but you can give it a shot— the ten- to twelve-inch-high foliage is very pretty on its own.

Light: For the best blooms, keep the plant in bright light, preferably with at least a few hours of direct sunlight.

Sustenance: They need a little drying out between watering so wait until the soil is pretty parched, then water plentifully.

Reproduction: Don't bother trying. They're grown from seed and will not reproduce with cuttings.

Troubleshooting: The amethyst violet can grow on the scraggly side, so pinch back often.

The Down and Dirty: The color of these flowers is so beautiful that it's best not to compete with a fancy pot. Stick to one color, a bleached-out white for example, and let the purple stand out.

Christmas Pepper

Even though you can't really eat them, they look just like the authentic red-hot ones. The plants themselves are approximately twelve inches tall and bushy with bright red oblong peppers, which appear for about two to three months in the late summer to early winter, then shrivel up and die. Since they're annuals, it's unlikely they'll flower again, so this is one plant that is probably better off going to horticultural heaven.

Light: Bright light with a few hours of direct sun is the best atmosphere for this plant. Without enough light, the leaves will wither and fall off.

Sustenance: Lots of water and keep it coming. Keep the soil moist but don't let it stand in water.

Reproduction: Forget about it.

Troubleshooting: A lack of humidity can cause the plant to lose its fruit earlier. Spritz it frequently or allow it to stand on moistened pebbles.

The Down and Dirty: They're very dramatic-looking on their own, but to increase the impact, group a few of them together in a large decorative container and use it as a centerpiece on your coffee table.

Cyclamen

This plant has rather odd-looking flowers that are shaped like a badminton birdie, with petals that fan out upward. The colors are spectacular—red, yellow, and pink are a few of the options, and they keep flowering for months, generally from winter through early spring. The flower stems grow to about nine inches, while the leaves cluster at about half that height.

Light: Cyclamen prefer bright indirect light; direct sun is likely to scorch their leaves.

Sustenance: Cyclamen are grown from tubers, which are similar to bulbs, and they can rot when water is poured directly onto them. Instead, fill a shallow bowl with water and place the cyclamen's container in the water. In a sort of upside-down watering technique, the soil will soak up as much water as it needs. After about ten minutes, remove the container and allow it to drain. Repeat when the soil becomes dry, most likely a few days later.

Reproduction: Nope. Though generally treated as annuals, with a little effort you can bring them back year after year. After the plant stops flowering, slowly decrease watering until the leaves turn yellow, at which point you stop watering completely. Put the entire pot in a closet or other dark, cool place until the early fall when you can bring it out, repot it, put it in bright light, and wait for it to come back to life. Don't feel bad if it doesn't. You did your best and they can be fickle.

Troubleshooting: As soon as the flowers die, pinch them off to make room for new growth. Do the same with the leaves, as a certain amount will probably yellow and die in the course of the plant's flowering life span.

The Down and Dirty: Of all the flowering plants, this is one of the easiest so it's a good confidence builder for a first-time gardener. Plant it in a container with some history—an aged copper pot or a chipped and faded terra-cotta container.

Kalanchoe

In the dead of winter, when you really need to see something besides brown tree branches and white snowdrifts, the vivid kalanchoe can offer you deliverance. The plants themselves grow to about fifteen inches, with tiny flower clusters in white, orange, pink, red, or yellow, which can bloom from fall straight through spring. Kalanchoes are considered annuals—once the flowers are gone, they're difficult to bring back.

Light: In order to get the best flowers, you should give the kalanchoe as much light as possible. It would prefer direct sun, but will do fine in a bright room.

Sustenance: Since kalanchoes are succulents (the leaves store water), they don't require a great deal of attention. Give them enough water to keep the soil moist and allow them to get fairly dry in between feedings.

Reproduction: You can propagate them through cuttings—simply insert the end of a two-inch-long leaf tip in soil—but there's very little chance that the new plant will produce flowers.

Troubleshooting: Since they're difficult to coax into flowering for a second year, a lot of people throw kalanchoes away after the flowers die. But kept in good condition, the foliage is an attractive shade of light green so it might be worth holding on to in its flower-free state.

The Down and Dirty: Its fortitude in the face of long, water-free days makes kalanchoe a good option for someone who wants the color without the responsibility.

TIP: The Smell of It

Half the pleasure of cut flowers is the aroma of a big fat rose or a delicate tulip. To put a little background fragrance in your home, plant something scented. Some of the flowers mentioned in this chapter that provide an odoriferous kick are primrose, gardenia, scented geraniums, and violets. Put fragrant plants in a spot with a lot of air circulation. This will spread the scent throughout your home.

The Next Level

If you're ready to take a stab at something slightly more challenging, get your hands on one of these bloomers.

Azalea

The flowers are big and beautiful and they perch atop clusters of bright green leaves. Like its cousin the rhododendron, the azalea's natural blooming cycle begins in mid-spring, but florists often force them at other times so you can find them almost year-round. Though they're considered annuals and some people will throw them away when they're done flowering, the foliage can be very pretty on its own and will grow to be about eighteen inches tall. While flowering the following year is not guaranteed, it does happen so you might as well give it a try.

Light: Though they prefer bright indirect light, they'll be okay with a few hours of direct sun. They will not flower in the shade.

Sustenance: Keep the soil moist throughout. Azaleas are very good at telling you when they're thirsty—their leaves will sag and begin to fall off.

Reproduction: Plant three-inch stem cuttings directly into a small, soil-filled pot. Keep the babies in a shady position until they root (about eight weeks), then move them into a new pot and place it near indirect light.

Troubleshooting: For some reason, azaleas hate water with lime; its leaves will begin to yellow and die. If this happens, feed it lime-free water (it doesn't necessarily have to be imported designer water). They also dislike heat and will begin to lose leaves. Move it to a cooler position.

The Down and Dirty: The azalea is also a classic gift plant, a great way to impress someone and force them to think about you year after year.

African Violet

For some reason, people seem to either have the African violet gene or they don't. If you're not one of the lucky ones, take heart, you just need to be extra diligent. African violets are usually (though not always) deep purple with a yellow center and have large dark green leaves that grow individually. They're perennials, and given the right conditions, the plant will flower continuously, each leaf growing to about six inches high.

Light: If it's too bright, the leaves will get scorched, so keep it in bright, but indirect sun.

Sustenance: Keep the soil moist but don't overdo it, as the roots will rot easily if overwatered. Allow the top few inches of soil to dry out between waterings.

People seem to either have the African violet gene or they don't.

Reproduction: Surprisingly simple to propagate, the African violet takes quickly to division. Remove one leaf (with the stalk) from the plant and trim it down with a sharp knife until it's about two inches long. Stick the bottom half of the stem in a small container with moistened soil, cover it with a plastic bag, and place the plant in bright indirect light. Within about eight weeks, a whole new plantlet should have formed at the base of the leaf.

Troubleshooting: Too much water or not enough humidity can make the plant sickly. If you become convinced you're not an African violet person and it looks as though it might be near the end, try to save it by propagating the leaves and giving them to friends.

The Down and Dirty: Keep it in a small, shallow, and unassuming container so the plant can speak for itself.

Bird-of-Paradise

This looks like one of those plants you see in tropical greenhouses, or maybe on movie sets—you know they're probably plastic because no normal human could grow something so surreal. Well, surprise! Reaching a height of up to four feet, this perennial not only looks amazing, with orange, purple, and red flowers shooting out from a host of lanky green leaves, it's also pretty easy to grow.

Light: Give it as much direct sunlight as possible. The more light, the more impressive and frequent the flowers.

Sustenance: When you water it, give it enough to thoroughly moisten the soil, but allow the top half or so to dry out between waterings.

Reproduction: Remove the plant from its container and gently separate three of the leaves, including some roots, from the rest. Plant them in another container. Put your new progeny in bright light and water moderately until the roots take, in about six weeks. Then give it direct sun and treat it like a regular plant, but don't expect flowers for two to three years.

Troubleshooting: Keep an eye out for scale, especially on the underside of leaves, as this plant is a particular favorite of these pests.

The Down and Dirty: Growing the bird-of-paradise without a lot of light is basically impossible, so don't fool yourself into thinking that the five-minute snatch of sunlight you get at noon will be sufficient. Its vertical climb is particularly impressive; if you want to make the most of it, plant it in a tall container.

Bougainvillea

Traditionally recognized as the plant with the bright pink flowers you see scaling walls in tropical climates, the bougainvillea can also be reined in and kept as an annual houseplant. Check your local nursery for the dwarf variety, which can flower from spring through the fall and, if not cut back, grow several feet tall. Be warned, however, that they are not the easiest plant to maintain and they need a very sunny spot to thrive.

Light: At least three hours of direct sunlight is necessary to induce the bougainvillea to bloom. Even in the off-months when it's resting, it should have warm temperatures and bright light.

Sustenance: When the plant is blooming, allow the top third of the soil to dry out between waterings. Cut back even further during the rest period, feeding it just enough to prevent the soil from drying out. Begin watering more freely in the spring, when it starts to show signs of life.

Reproduction: Unless you have a climate-controlled greenhouse tucked away behind your bedroom, fuhgeddahboutit.

Troubleshooting: Keep in mind that it is an extremely fussy plant. It tends to lose a lot of leaves during the winter, and if it's not feeling perfectly at ease with its environmental conditions, can drop leaves in the spring and summer as well. Lack of sun and warmth are the most common problems.

The Down and Dirty: Bougainvillea grows so quickly that it makes ivy look lethargic. In the summer, you could plant it in a container on the floor and train it up a trellis around the window to create a sort of frame, or plant it in a carved urn and let it spill out over the sides.

Calamondin Orange

Though you're not likely to yield a round of screwdrivers, these grape-sized fruits can churn out some excellent orangeade. Growing up to four feet tall, this perennial does look just like a miniature orange tree though, with fragrant flowers, lush foliage, and scattered fruit that turns from green to orange as it ripens.

Light: Lots of it; this plant needs at least four hours of direct sun a day and prefers temperatures on the cool side, between 60 to 70°F.

Sustenance: Add fertilizer every two weeks and allow the top half of the soil to dry out between waterings during the summer when it's bearing fruit; when it's hibernating, water it just enough to prevent it from getting too parched, and skip the fertilizer.

Reproduction: Most citrus trees grow pretty easily from seed. Planted in the spring, the calamondin orange should germinate in about six weeks. Keep it out of direct sunlight for about two months, then treat it as a regular tree. Nurtured well, it should grow fairly quickly into a nice-looking foliage plant, though it might take as long as ten years to bear fruit.

Troubleshooting: Citrus trees are especially susceptible to pests. Keep a lookout for spider mites and scale on the underside of leaves.

The Down and Dirty: Trim back the leaves fairly often to encourage the tree to get full and bushy. Since you've started out with a tropical touch, why not take it all the way and plant the tree in either a brightly colored Miami Beach–inspired pot or a whitewashed terra-cotta container.

Carpet Plant

This bright-foliaged annual tends to propagate itself and spread rapidly, hence its name. The leaves on most species are dark green with light veins running through; small, delicate flowers sprout out among them. They grow to about four inches, flower throughout the warm months, and will come back the following year with little fuss.

Light: The carpet plant needs a fair amount of bright light and thrives with a few hours of direct light, as long as it's not too hot.

Sustenance: Keep the soil moist and add a tiny dose of fertilizer at least once a week.

Reproduction: It's surprisingly easy, considering it's a flowering plant, because the leaves that make contact with the soil will put down their own roots. Just cut a section away from the mother plant and transfer it to its own home.

Troubleshooting: The carpet plant does best in humid conditions. If the leaves start to fade out, it might not be getting enough moisture or the sun might be too intense. Since they are prolific reproducers, they need frequent trimming or annual repotting.

The Down and Dirty: Since it tends to keep its roots near the surface, the best containers for the carpet plant are shallow. Its abundance also looks good in hanging pots.

Chrysanthemum

In the wild, chrysanthemums grow several feet tall, but nurseries can trick domestic versions of these annuals into stunted growth patterns. The puffy flowers can be white, yellow, pink, or orange with several little petals surrounding a central, often yellow, disk.

Light: They prefer bright light but temperatures on the cool side.

Sustenance: For some reason, chrysanthemums tend to dry out quickly, so be attentive with the watering can.

Reproduction: They're pretty difficult to duplicate, and while you can keep them around to try to coax them into another year of flowering, they have a tendency to get long and stringy.

Troubleshooting: Many of the stems on your chrysanthemum might try to produce just one large flower. It might look nice but once it's gone you've pretty much blown the wad. Pinch back that one flower when it's still in the budding stages. This will encourage side shoots and more—though smaller—flowers.

The Down and Dirty: The flowers may be bright and showy, but chrysanthemums tend to look best in bulk. Fill a simple container with two or more groupings for a bountiful effect.

Fuchsia

This bushy perennial looks fake from a distance because of the intensely colored, bell-like flowers. The blooms can be anything from hot pink to white to purple and they grow in clusters. Some fuchias are trailers and will grow up to a foot long; the dwarf variety will stall at about six inches.

Light: Fuchsias need extra bright light, with as much direct sun as possible, preferably at least three hours, or they will not bloom.

Sustenance: They're also particularly greedy when it comes to water so give them enough to keep the soil moist without letting them stand in water.

Reproduction: Take cuttings four inches long from just below a leaf node. Strip off the lower leaves and plant the cuttings in a small container. Enclose them in a plastic bag and wait for them to root, about three weeks, then repot and place your new plant in direct sunlight

Troubleshooting: If you want to keep your fuchsia after its flowering period is over—usually by early winter—cut it back by about half so it will have the energy to flower again the following season.

The Down and Dirty: If you equate hanging baskets with restaurants staffed by singing waiters (or something similar), fine;

keep it on a table where it can spill over the edges. Otherwise, strap it up by a window and let it dangle.

TIP: Spread the Wealth

Whether you're cutting back a flowering plant to induce more growth or when you just feel the urge, clip a few flowers and transfer them to a vase in your bathroom, kitchen, or any other spot in your home that doesn't get enough light to have a plant of its own.

Primrose

Tiny little flower clusters in pink, red, yellow, or white spring out of big leaf clumps, and in some species the whole plant is covered with a fine white powder. The dainty effect of these annuals brightens up the late winter months, when they're generally in bloom. Most varieties will grow to be about fifteen inches tall.

Light: They prefer a few hours of direct sun, but can make do in a spot which is generally bright.

Sustenance: Primoses can be fickle—they are thirsty and prefer damp soil but are quick to complain when they get too much moisture. Fertilize every two weeks.

Reproduction: They're very difficult to reproduce, and in fact, are best grown from seed. If you decide on that route, plant in the spring to achieve winter flowers. To make your old plant flower again, keep it cool and shaded in the summer and allow the soil to dry out slightly.

Troubleshooting: To make the flowers last as long as possible, keep the plant in a cool room—50 to 55°F is ideal. Pick off dead and dying flowers to force the plant to produce more. If the leaves start to yellow, put some Epsom salts in the water.

The Down and Dirty: The rather delicate appearance of the primrose is best shown off in small doses. Put one cluster in a miniature pot and use it as a table centerpiece.

Living Room Shrubs

There is a wide variety of flowering shrubs, which are basically bushy plants; if kept well-pruned, they can be great decorative touches. Depending on their size and how they're pruned, many of these shrubs are indistinguishable from your garden-variety houseplants. The difference, however, is that given the right conditions and space, they can fill out and grow up to six feet high. Unfortunately, most of these shrubs are difficult to propogate. Even if you can induce cuttings to root, it is highly unlikely that they'll ever produce flowers. Most thrive in cooler temperatures and higher humidity, so if you prefer your home on the overheated side, shrubs are probably not for you.

Gardenia

Their white fragrant flowers tend to bloom in the summer months, but the rest of the year the rich green foliage is nothing to sneeze at. In the wild, gardenia shrubs can grow up to six feet high, but when confined they rarely exceed two feet. Keep them in bright, but not direct light with temperatures on the cool side—around 65°F. Overwatering is a surefire death inducer; allow the top half of the soil to dry out between visits. To keep it looking tidy, prune back any gangly foliage (carefully avoiding buds) in the spring before it flowers.

Hydrangea

This is one of those beautiful plants to enjoy while its blooming; then, unless you're very diligent about keeping it cool (between 60 to 65°F), resign yourself to owning a beautiful piece of foliage. Indoors, it's very difficult to induce the large showy flower clusters to make an appearance the following year, though it's not out of the question. Hydrangeas are available in blue, purple, pink, or white. They flower in spring and may stay colorful for up to eight weeks, growing up to two feet. Bright, indirect sun, and moist soil will bring on the best results.

Oleander

One of the hardier of the shrubs, oleander is fairly easy to grow, as long as you have direct sunlight year-round. It can grow up to six feet and puts out clusters of white, pink, red, or yellow flowers, usually in the summer. It needs moderate water and can be reproduced pretty easily through stem cuttings. However, this is not a good option for those with young children or curious pets because oleander is poisonous if eaten.

Rhododendron

It generally produces white or pink flowers in springtime, though nurseries often train them to bloom in the winter. When they're flowering, rhododendrons prefer bright, indirect light; afterward, tone down the sun factor and put them in a spot with medium light, like a north-facing window. They also prefer cool conditions and might start shedding quickly if it's too warm for them. Peat moss will probably give you better results than ordinary soil, as the roots need to be kept very moist for the shrub to thrive. Humidity is also key; if possible, set the container on a tray of pebbles.

TIP: The Crowded Container

There is no rule that says you have to limit your container to a single plant. Group a few together for extra impact. Make sure the container is large enough for all of the roots and go crazy. Try ferns with flowers; put some ground cover—plants that stay low to the ground and tend to spread quickly—in the base of your tree's home. Toss together plants with various textures, heights, and colors, even those you wouldn't expect as roommates. Just make sure their light and watering needs are compatible.

Window Boxes

No matter where you live, as long as you have windows and windowsills, you can create window boxes. From afar, they can look intimidating, with all those colors and textures spilling out everywhere, but the irony is that some of the best ones are created by people who have absolutely no idea of what they're doing. You could plot and plan what to put where and create something worthy of framing. Or you could toss in whatever looks good and end up with a chaotic masterpiece, which can be more appealing than any self-conscious creation.

Getting Started

The best time to put together a window box is in the spring, when seedlings are readily available and you have the whole summer to let your concoction turn into a lush mass of green. All you need is a window box, dirt, and an armload of seedlings or plants.

The window box can be plastic, wood, or clay—the only essentials are drainage holes, since you have no way of controlling how much water it will collect. Window box is a generic term, it doesn't even have to be a box; you could use a regular pot or any other shape you want. If your windowsills aren't wide enough to make you

If your windowsills aren't wide enough to make you confident that the whole concoction isn't going to tumble down onto someone's head....

confident that the whole concoction isn't going to tumble down to the ground (or if you're up a few floors, onto someone's head), there are brackets you can attach to the building for support.

The Ingredients

Before you buy the stuffing materials, consider your light. If the window has northern exposure you should look for species that can thrive without direct sun, though even light bounced off other sources, such as grass or windows across the street, will be enough for most.

Annuals are the most common choice for window boxes. They're pretty, they bloom wildly, and they last the summer. You could choose perennials or biennials as well, but if you want them to live through the winter you'll probably have to bring them inside since the depth of dirt in a container is not going to be enough to withstand the freezing temperatures of most regions' winters.

Other than making sure to pick plants with similar water and light needs, go crazy in your choices. Think about colors and leaf textures and shapes and toss a bunch in the same container. Ivy is a great choice because it grows like a weed and will spill over the side and make your neighbors think you know what you're doing. Mix spiky textures with smooth rounded ones, tall plants with trailing ones. Be very generous in your allocation and pack them in tight so it looks like a massive plant party.

Putting It Together

You might want to do a little experimentation before you commit to a design. Fill the container halfway with soil and remove your plants from their containers. Shove them in together and move them around until you like how they look. Don't worry about losing some dirt or a little root breakage, they'll survive. When you've got it just the way you want, fill in the empty spaces between the plants with extra soil and pat it down. Water the window box until water comes out of the drainage holes and put it on display.

Keep It Going

To ensure yourself a full season of color, pretty much all you have to do is pinch off dead flowers, add some fertilizer once in a while, and water generously, especially if it's in the sun (though part of the beauty of the window box is that, thanks to nature, in a good year your watering responsibilities can be cut in half).

TIP: Overheated

If you live in a hot climate, or your window box receives intense summer sun, keep in mind that dark colors attract more heat. Therefore, to decrease the chances of your plants shriveling up in overheated agony, opt for a light-colored container.

The Mainstays

Don't limit yourself. Experiment with a number of different plants and combinations. But here are some classic window box ingredients to get you started:

Flowers	Greens
Marigolds	Ferns
Pansies	Baby's breath
Impatiens	Parsley
Petunias	Coleus
Begonias	Ivy

Fruits and vegetables also make great window box ingredients. Tomatoes, peppers, and strawberries in particular are good bets because they're not greedy with their root space. Combine them with flowers and greens for a well-rounded creation.

chapter five

Urban Hunting and Gathering

Home Grown

There's really nothing like the satisfaction of eating something you've grown yourself, even if you can swallow the lion's share of it in a bite or two. A home-grown tomato is somehow sweeter and juicier than the store-bought variety; herbs have more zest.

Pretty much any vegetable or herb is going to need a lot of direct sunlight and most will also appreciate some fresh air, which is why herbs and vegetables make good window box ingredients. There's also a pretty good chance that not all of your seeds will take root, so increase your odds of success by planting more than just a few. You can always thin them out later.

A Mixed Salad

Surprise! You probably thought container gardeners were limited to growing ordinary houseplants and the occasional tree. Well don't go swearing off the local grocery store yet, but you could whip up a couple of salads with the fixings of a window box or two. Dwarf vegetables are designed specifically for containers; many other veggies just need a good deep pot to churn out the produce.

If you're growing from seed, start anywhere from early March to late April, depending on how long the plant takes to produce and when you want to start snacking.

Beans

The pole variety sprouts and spreads very quickly over a trellis or other support, and should ideally be planted in a window box type of container that's long and deep. If you don't have the space, opt for bush beans and plant them in a regular pot at least a foot deep.

Getting Started: You can either plant seeds directly in their container or nurse them to seedling size in a smaller vessel, then move them to their final destination. In either case, make sure

There's really nothing like the satisfaction of eating something you've grown yourself.

the soil is damp when you sow the seeds, then lay off the water until the seedlings emerge.

Care and Feeding: When the beans reach a height of about six inches, begin fertilizing and continue every two weeks. Attach pole beans to a trellis so they won't collapse. Given the opportunity, they can grow to several feet. In order to thrive, beans need full sun, warm temperatures, and damp soil. They should be ready to harvest in about two months.

Broccoli

Whether or not you actually like to eat it, broccoli is one of the easier vegetables to grow, and as your mother undoubtedly told you, a good counterbalance to a junk food diet.

Getting Started: Grow it from seeds or seedlings, planting them about ten inches apart. It will take about two months from seed to table, so plant in the spring for an early summer crop, or later if you'd prefer to harvest in autumn.

Care and Feeding: Keep the soil moist without letting it get soggy and give it as much direct sun as possible. Water generously and fertilize about once a month. Each plant should produce one large cluster of broccoli; after you've picked it, the side leaves should produce smaller, baby clusters.

Carrots

Unless you've got an awfully deep container, you should stick with the miniature versions.

Getting Started: They're remarkably easy to grow from seed, just plant to the depth listed on the package. Though they're not especially breathtaking in appearance, sending out the same bushy ends you see on the store-bought variety, they're best grown in a window box or other container with straight sides. Most of the smaller versions will be ready to eat about six weeks after planting, so if you want a carrot-filled summer, keep planting more seeds at two-week intervals.

Care and Feeding: You'll get the best results from full sun, at least two hours a day. Keep the soil moist and fertilize about once a month. They're ready to be picked when the above-ground leafy part gets to about an inch or two in diameter.

Corn

You really don't need a field in Iowa to produce a few diminutive foot-high ears. Midget corn is specially mutated to be a container plant, though you still need a pretty deep pot—a large wooden barrel for example.

Getting Started: Corn grows pretty quickly from seed, but you can pick up seedlings from a nursery. If you grow from seed, plant them in starter containers and stick in a warm, dark spot until they germinate. Then move them to a large container, placing them about six inches apart. Since each transplant stalk will only produce one ear, if you want a more continuous stock of corn, stagger the planting throughout the spring.

Care and Feeding: Place the container in full sunlight and start fertilizing monthly when the plants are about six inches tall. Keep the soil moist, but not soaked. You should have fully developed midget ears in about a month.

Cucumbers

Surprisingly easy to cultivate, cucumbers grow off vines you can attach to a trellis stuck into the pot. Be warned, however, that they can grow several feet tall, so if you're low on vertical space, pick out a dwarf variety.

Getting Started: Start the seeds in the spring. Cucumbers are a unique vegetable in that they actually prefer cool temperatures, so, provided you're past "cloudy breath" weather, you could even put them out on a windowsill. When the seedlings get a few inches high, transplant them to a container.

Care and Feeding: Begin fertilizing when the sprouts are about six inches tall and place them in full sun. Keep the soil moist; if they're underwatered, cucumbers can taste slightly bitter. The vines will grow fairly quickly, so keep an eye on them to be sure they're not overtaking the trellis. Your crop should start showing up after about two months. Pick cucumbers immediately or the adults will hog all the nourishment from any subsequent produce.

Lettuce

Greens are pretty easy to grow; most varieties do well in a pot or window box. Line up a series of your favorite lettuces—romaine, butter, red leaf, oak leaf—in a single container.

Getting Started: Plant transplants or seeds in the early spring directly in the container. The distance between each will depend on the variety you're growing and how big you want them to get before picking. Check the seed packet for the ideal depth.

Care and Feeding: Though they can stand direct sun, most types of lettuce prefer more indirect or reflected light. Keep the soil moist and fertilize the plants every two weeks. If you grow them from seed, they should reach full lettuce size in about two to three months. There's no rule stating you have to wait that long, however, and you can pick them whenever the number of leaves fits your appetite.

Onions and Scallions

You're not going to get the mammoth variety you see in the supermarket, but you can grow a good number of diminutive onions or scallions.

Getting Started: They grow pretty quickly from seed and you'll get the best results if you plant them in a shallow (about four inches deep) starter container early in the spring. When the shoots get to about four inches tall, transplant them to a larger container, making sure to leave a few inches in between each seedling.

Care and Feeding: Keep the soil moist and begin fertilizing about a month after planting, then continue about once a month. Onions and scallions will do well with either full sun or partial shade and should produce in about two months.

Peppers

The perfect container vegetable, peppers are easy to grow and they look good doing it. You can grow almost any type of pepper—hot or sweet, elongated or bell.

Getting Started: Transplant a nursery-bought seedling or grow peppers directly from seed. If you decide to go the seed route, start in March or April for a July pepper fest. Follow the directions on the seed packet to determine how deep and far apart they should be planted.

Care and Feeding: Give peppers as much sun as you can and fertilize once a month. Allowing the soil to dry out slightly between waterings helps speed the maturing process. The plant will grow to about a foot tall—you can pick them when they're green or wait a bit and most will ripen to a deep red. From just one plant, you should be able to eke out an entire season's worth of peppers.

Potatoes

It's the classic elementary school project—stick a potato in the dirt and watch the sprouts emerge. New potatoes tend to work best, but you can try this with any variety.

Getting Started: This works best with a large container, one that leaves room for the baby taters to form. Buy some potatoes in the early spring and sit them on end, "eye" side up, until they sprout. To hurry the process along, stick the potato in a jar of water, propping it up with toothpicks, so just the bottom half is immersed. Roots should pop out within a week. Fill the bottom of the container with about three inches of soil and stick the potatoes in, sprout side up, roots in the ground, leaving about six inches between potatoes. Cover them with more soil, and water just enough to dampen the soil. They should root within a few weeks.

Care and Feeding: Put the container in a sunny spot and keep the soil moist. Water frequently and fertilize every two weeks. When the first flowers appear on the plants, you're ready for your initial harvest. Feel around in the dirt for the largest potatoes and leave the other ones to keep growing. When the foliage starts to yellow, it's time to harvest the rest—each initial potato should yield several babies.

Squash

It grows big—and quickly! The normal garden variety squash needs a lot of root space so look for smaller varieties, like bush summer squash, and a large container.

Getting Started: Start the seeds in a warm dark spot and transplant, one to a container, when the seedlings are a few inches high.

Care and Feeding: Place the plants in full sun and, when they're about six inches tall, start fertilizing every two weeks. Water frequently and abundantly, keeping the soil as moist as possible without letting it get soggy. It should grow to about one to two feet tall and begin producing fruit in about one and a half to two months.

Strawberries

They're surprisingly easy to grow as long as you have good drainage and adequate sunlight.

Getting Started: They can be grown from seed, but you're better off starting with transplants you order through a catalog or pick up at the local nursery. Strawberry jars—tall containers often made of terra-cotta with a number of small openings on the sides—provide the perfect housing, though you can also use any other deep container. Fill the jar with dampened soil to within a few inches of the top and add handfuls of soil to the side openings (they jut out slightly to provide a platform). Put a strawberry plant in each opening and a few in the top. Water thoroughly and place in full sunlight.

Care and Feeding: Fertilize every few weeks and water often to keep it from drying out. The plants will spread to cover the pot with lush greenery and flowers, which will eventually turn into strawberries. Since they bear fruit in the spring, it's probably going to be a year before you're pulling the powdered sugar out of your pantry.

TIP: Multiuse Pot

It's called a strawberry pot but by no means should it be limited only to strawberries. You can plant just about anything in one, and they actually look best when packed with a mishmash of plants, including herbs and flowers and foliage. Use a variety of colors and textures for the most interesting results.

Tomatoes

Take your pick—most tomatoes will do just fine in a deep pot. Due to their diminutive nature, cherry tomatoes make great container specimens, as do patio tomatoes, a breed specially formulated for small spaces.

Getting Started: Although it seems like a daunting concept, it's not difficult to grow tomatoes from seeds. When started in early spring (six to eight weeks before the last frost of the year), they germinate in about three to four weeks, and will grow in sturdy form if given enough light. Plant them directly in the container, treating them as you would any seed. Keep the container sheltered from light and the soil moist until seedlings form. Then douse with sunlight. They're going to need a fair amount of space to spread out and bear fruit (the tomato is known botanically as a fruit, but it's used as a vegetable) so when they get a few inches high, thin them out.

Or pick up a seedling or developed plant at a local nursery and repot it in a large container. Keep it alone or pack a few herbs and flowers in the same pot. Basil makes a nice complement, and hints of salads to come.

Care and Feeding: Keep the soil moist and fertilize the tomatoes every two weeks. As the plant grows, it might need some support to keep it from toppling over. You could either buy a tomato cage, which is a wire brace you stick in the soil around the plant, or you could secure the stem to a wooden stake. Simply stick the stake into the soil next to the tomato stem and use a twist tie to attach them. The plant will develop little yellow flowers, which will eventually evolve into tomatoes. Pick them as soon as they ripen; they should start showing up about two months after the original planting date.

TIP: Tomato Decoy

Tomatoes are very susceptible to whiteflies, which will quickly suck the life out of them. They're incredibly hard to get rid of so it's best to avoid them in the first place by planting marigolds, which for some reason work as pest repellents, in the same pot.

Future Harvests

Sometimes you just have to wait for a good thing. That's the case with most of these plants, grown from seeds, pits, and nuts. Most will take several years—from two to ten or more—to actually reward your efforts with edibles, but in the meantime, the foliage is good looking and you can get all smug when you disclose the plant's origins.

Since most fruit that you buy in the grocery store is some sort of hybrid cross, it's not guaranteed that the resulting tree will bear more fruit. You might have better luck with produce straight from the farmer's market.

Avocado

Suspend the avocado pit in a glass of water, using toothpicks, so that the bottom of the pit is just below liquid level. Place it in a low-light, warm location until it splits to reveal a shoot and roots, then move it to a sunnier location. When the root structure begins to develop, plant it in soil with the top of the pit just sticking out. Water enough to keep soil moist and fertilize every few weeks. If you want it to grow into a tree rather than just a bushy plant, pinch out the top growth every few weeks so side branches will form. Litchis and mangos are grown in basically the same way, though they prefer the air to be a bit more tropical.

Nuts

Peanuts, acorns, chestnuts, walnuts, and pine nuts—pretty much any nut—can be plopped in a pot of soil and enticed to grow with direct sun and lots of water. When you're gathering the nuts, look for ones that have already started to sprout; this will speed the process. Plant the nut about an inch deep and don't be too ambitious with pot size, at least to start. A container about four inches deep will allow the roots to grow without overwhelming them with the possibilities.

Pineapple

Who'd have thought that even in the coldest climates you could grow your own little taste of the tropics. Slice off the top of the pineapple, making sure to leave about an inch of the fruit attached, then trim off the outer flesh until you're left with just the center core. Let it dry for a couple of days, then strip off the bottom leaves and stick it in damp soil so that the top leaves are sticking out. Give it plenty of light and humidity but lay off on the water, giving it only enough to keep it moist until it grows roots. Once it's started growing, treat it like a regular plant, keeping the soil moist and fertilizing every few weeks. It will grow long spiky leaves and, with luck and diligence, present its very own offspring attached to a stem.

Pomegranate

The adult pomegranate has a sort of bushlike appearance, with light green leaves and bright red flowers. Prepare a few seeds for procreation by drying them out in a dark place. In the spring, plant one per pot in small containers, about an inch deep in soil. After they've sprouted, give them plenty of sunshine and ample water. Repot them as they appear to outgrow their homes.

The Pits (Cherry and Peach)

Very easy to grow, they make beautiful plants, then bushes, then trees—limited in size only by the size of their containers—even if they do take several years of sunny and warm conditions to bear fruit. Plant the pit in soil and keep in low light conditions until it germinates (be patient, it could take several weeks). When it sprouts, move it to a sunny location, fertilize it monthly, and water generously. Repot whenever it dwarfs its surroundings.

Citrus

For some reason, lemons and grapefruits tend to work the best, but they usually don't bear fruit until they reach about six feet tall. Still, their foliage is dark and full and provides a handsome touch of warmth in a sunny window. Plant the seeds in dampened soil, and keep the container in a warm dark place until the shoots appear. When they're several inches high, transplant the seedlings to individual containers and move them to a sunny place. Water generously, fertilize monthly, and repot when the roots have filled the container.

Dates

Though you're not likely to get a large date harvest any time soon (or ever, really), the date stone will fan out into a date palm, and in several years will become a large palm tree several feet tall. Plant the stone directly into damp soil and keep it warm and dark until the first indications of life appear, generally in about a month. Then move the pot to a sunny location and fertilize it monthly. Water generously and repot every year or so, whenever it looks cramped.

TIP: Think Thin

Though crowds can be a good thing for flowers and window boxes, most edibles—fruits and vegetables especially—need space to churn out their produce. If you're planting from seed, make sure to thin them out when they reach about four to six inches high. The space you leave between seedlings depends on the size of the eventual plant. In general, if you want to grow flowers in the same container with edibles, you have more leeway since the flowers tend to be more conservative with their root space.

Herbs and Spices

In addition to being kitchen staples, herbs can also provide a great decorative touch to an otherwise dull container. They're not big root-space hogs, so you can pack a whole variety together in one window box or wedge them in next to some flowers. They can get pretty scraggly as they grow, so keep them cut back and use the cuttings for potpourri or cooking. Or stick a bunch of them in a glass bottle, fill it with olive oil and give it as a gift—better yet use it yourself. Though some could endure the winter if brought inside, you're better off treating them all as annuals and starting fresh the following spring.

You can use it in all types of salads and pastas or wow
your friends and make homemade pesto.

Basil

If you're not a big basil fan, you will be by the time you're halfway through the growing season. You can use it in all types of salads and pastas or wow your friends and make homemade pesto. It needs moist soil and a lot of direct sunlight, but once it's started it grows like a weed so you should have plenty to last you the summer. Grow it from seed and fertilize every two weeks once it's a few inches high. When flowers appear, you might be tempted to admire them, but don't. When herbs flower it sends them into decline so pinch them off immediately. Also pinch back leaves occasionally to make the whole plant bushier. At the end of the season, have yourself a basil fiesta because it won't last through the winter.

If you're a big basil fan, fill a big pot with different varieties (globe, purple leaf, sweet), otherwise group it with tomatoes or other herbs. For an Italian touch, plant it in a recycled sixteen-ounce tomato can so you'll remember what to do with it once it's grown.

TIP: Salad in a Pot

Make things even easier for yourself and plant a container with all the fixings for a salad. Include a tomato plant, basil, and some other herbs, like parsley. In addition to furnishing a one-stop salad bar, the combination of different colors and textures make for great eye candy.

Catnip

Stop being so selfish and think of someone else for a change. Given the chance (which is generally doubtful), catnip will fill out into a bushy plant and grow to be about twelve inches. Keep the soil moist but not too wet, and put it in a sunny location. One word of advice: If Fluffy's an ardent fan of catnip, plant it in a nonbreakable container.

Chives

These long thin tubes are nothing spectacular to look at, so plant them next to something showier. But their garlicky taste really spices up eggs or a salad. Grow them from seeds or seedlings and fertilize every two weeks. Relatively hardy, chives can thrive with minimal sun. The soil should be kept moist. Snip off the ends whenever you need them.

Dill

It looks like a mixture between a fern and a Christmas tree, with the added benefit of being an excellent addition to meat, fish, and soup. Plant it from seed, keep it in a sunny location with damp soil, and fertilize every two weeks until flowers appear. This is one herb that should flower; the clusters of yellow blooms make it more attractive and tastier. Clip off portions at any time, though it's best picked just as the flowers are opening.

Garlic

The smell spreads a bit, but if you can stand that you can grow your own supply of the cooking staple. Fill a deep container with soil and plant the separated cloves, husks removed, end up, about six inches apart and two inches deep. Keep it moist and in a dark place until you see growth; then move it to a spot with full sun or part shade. Fertilize monthly and when the leafy tops look like they're sagging—usually about six weeks after planting—they're ready to harvest.

Mint

Choose your favorite—spearmint, peppermint, 'Chocolate Mint', apple, or orange mint—and then pick up some transplants and watch them multiply. It grows like a weed, spreading out and up, so keep cutting it back to make it full, healthy looking and under control. Drop a leaf or two in iced tea or use it as a garnish on soups or meat.

Mint's fortitude makes it one of the easiest herbs to grow; it will tolerate more shade than many other species. Fertilize every two weeks and water plentifully.

> **TIP: Herb Sampler**
>
> If you want to try a whole variety of herbs, try growing them in one of those cement blocks with a number of square holes in them. Plant one herb in each division and place the whole thing on a piece of screen large enough to catch all the dirt. It's a great way to keep them separate, especially if you get confused as to which herb is which—just draw a diagram.

Oregano

You might not be bowled over by its impressive foliage, but oregano makes a great trailer, spilling over the edges of the container and spicing up the surrounding air. It's best grown from transplants and prefers moist soil, a sunny location, and monthly fertilizing. Cut back the ends to encourage bushy growth and snip flowers as soon as they appear.

Parsley

Though this ubiquitous garnish is slow to grow from seed, transplants will fill out quickly and provide a season of meal decoration. Take your pick—flat Italian versus crunchier curly. Water generously, fertilize monthly, and put it in a spot with lots of sun.

Rosemary

All you have to do is rub your hand across the top of it to appreciate rosemary's musky aroma. It looks like a segment of a pine tree, but grows quickly and branches out in all directions. Use it in a potpourri or to season fish, meat, or vegetables. It's best grown from transplants and is one of the few herbs that can endure through the winter fairly easily (though if your plant doesn't last, just start over next year). Put it in full sun and allow it to dry out slightly between waterings. Fertilize once a month. Clip sprigs whenever you want; within a few days the spot you clipped will have two or more new directions of growth.

Sage

Another hardy herb, sage can also tough it through the winter. Any of the countless varieties (purple-leaf, golden, tricolor, etc.) are best grown from transplants. Their leaves have a strong woody fragrance and add a new dimension to lamb and poultry. Put it in a sunny location and allow the soil to dry out slightly between waterings. Fertilize once a month.

Tarragon

Its dark green leaves packed tight on thick woody branches provide continuous air freshening. Grow it from transplants and use tarragon in vinegars and salads. Put it in a sunny location, keep the soil moist, and fertilize once a month.

Thyme

It's another fragrant herb with weedlike growing patterns. Grow it from seed or transplant and use it on meat and poultry. Thyme prefers full sun, monthly fertilizing, and a break to dry out between waterings.

Edible Blooms

You're not going to get a four-course meal out of them, but edible flowers add a hint of color and taste to anything from salads to cakes. They come in pretty much any color you could imagine and each has a distinct flavor to it.

- Calendula have big floppy petals and a slightly tangy taste. They also make a splashy arrangement as cut flowers.

- Little did you know you could eat your carnations after the prom. They have a flavor somewhat like cloves and foliage in pink, red, yellow, and white. Another flower with similar flavor, though somewhat smaller flowers and denser foliage is dianthus.

- Marigolds, especially the lemon variety, are often used as a substitute for saffron. Plus they're incredibly easy to grow and help repel pests from your vegetables.

- The classic edible flower is the nasturtium with its bright colors and peppery flavor. The flowers are splashy and incredibly fragrant. Mix them with greens to dress up a salad or sprinkle them over cheese or soup.

- The sweetness and slight wintergreen flavor of sweet violets makes them a great dessert garnish. The deep violet leaves are surrounded by heart-shaped foliage.

chapter six

Help! It's Dying!

Horticultural First Aid

First of all, there's not a gardener
in the world who hasn't killed a
plant or two, so don't let any
green-thumbed snobs give
you grief about your wilted
leaves. There are, however, a
few things to look out for and
some steps you can take to
revive an ailing plant.

Before you panic and start looking
for a plant cemetery, take the plant off
to its own intensive care room so it
can't spread whatever's ailing it. Then
look it over from top to bottom. Check
the soil for obvious crawling things
and examine the tops and undersides of all the leaves. The cause
of its droopy disposition might be something obvious, like over-
crowded roots creeping out the top of the container.

Unfortunately, the root of the problem (excuse the pun) is not
always going to be so clear-cut. If you've closely examined the
plant and found no sign of pests, it's most likely a disease that's
wreaking havoc. Diseases are generally caused by some sort of
problem with the general conditions—lack of humidity or insufficient ventilation, for example. In those cases, once you figure
out the source of the problem, solving it can be a pretty simple
adjustment (unless you bought a tropical plant for a cold climate,
in which case you're going to have to either allow it to winter in
Florida with your grandparents or pack up your bags and move).

After isolating the sick plant, remove all dead and dying parts,
even if that means cutting your lush specimen down to a few
straggly stems. The sick parts are never going to get better and if
you can keep the rest healthy, it just might bounce back.

Preventive Measures

Pests and disease can strike even the most pampered plants, but there are some steps you can take to avoid these plagues. First of all, when you recycle soil make sure it was previously surrounding a healthy plant. If, heaven forbid, your plant dies, bury the soil with the corpse so you don't spread disease to the next inhabitant of the container. Also, immediately remove any dead or yellowed leaves from seemingly healthy plants as they could catch and spread infections.

Whether the previous tenant was sick or healthy, you should also scrub out your pot before putting in a new plant. As your mother might have said, you just never know what sort of filthy germs lie dormant, just waiting for their prey.

Cut flowers from the florist, as admittedly lovely as they are, are also notorious pest and disease transporters. Keep them away from your potted specimens and throw them away immediately after they've had their day.

TIP: Clean Sweep

As your mother may or may not have told you, the best defense against disease is cleanliness. In urban areas especially, dust and dirt can congregate on the leaves and stems, clogging the plants' pores and hindering their circulation. Periodically (as often as you think about it and are so inclined) wash the leaves with clean, room temperature water. Small plants can be dipped in a tub of water and swished around. Clean the foliage of larger leaves with a damp sponge or mister.

After the bath, make sure to wipe the plant as dry as possible. Too much water sitting on the leaves and foliage can lead to all sorts of trouble, including scorching from the sun and growth of bacteria, which can lead straight to disease.

Death by Drowning

Despite all the joking about the forgetful caretaker, one of the most common houseplant killers is too much water. Too much water prevents air from reaching the plant's roots, causing them to stop growing and eventually rot away. When in doubt, you're better off holding back on the nourishment rather than drowning the poor thing. Very few plants are going to need daily attention; two to three times a week is a much better guideline, though you should get your fingers dirty and actually feel the soil before making that call. If it feels dry below the surface, it's probably time to think about getting the watering can (though each plant is different so check the watering guidelines).

Signs of too little water include a gap between the dirt and the side of the container where the soil has literally shrunken. The soil might also become hard and cakey or begin to crack.

Another good gauge as to its hydra-health is how heavy the plant is. Pick it up before you water it, then again afterward; get used to how heavy it feels both ways. That way you'll be able to estimate its needs without getting a fingernail full of soil.

Some possible clues that you're overwatering include: leaves that turn yellow or brown, droop or fall off, or signs of algae growing on the pot or in the soil.

Running Hot and Cold

As much as most plants love a slight shift in temperature from day to evening, dramatic changes are a bad thing, which can cause the plant to drop its leaves and flower buds. Some ferns will become slightly blackened by unexpectedly cold temperatures; other plants will droop.

Avoid a situation where the climate is air-conditioned and cold by day and warmer at night, as this can throw plants into a complete tizzy. And keep all plants away from drafty windows; don't put them between the window and the curtain, especially at night.

And keep all plants away from drafty windows; don't put them
between the window and the curtain.

Effects and Possible Causes

Yellow Leaves

The number one sign of overwatering. Pinch off the yellow leaves and leave the plant alone for a few days to let it dry out. Then start watering sparsely and make sure you dump out any water that runs through the drainage holes.

Yellowing leaves can also be a sign that the plant is receiving an overabundance of light, either in bulk or intensity. If you've got it sitting on a sunny, south-facing windowsill, make sure that is what it really wants.

Brown or Yellow Spots

Generally caused by too much water splashing the leaves; water that's too cold is especially bad. Try to avoid the foliage when you're watering the plant, and focus instead on the roots. When you mist for humidity, make sure the water is room temperature and the mist is a fine one. Remember, you're trying to create humidity, not a rainstorm, so spray lightly.

The Droops

Few things are sadder-looking than a plant with seriously sagging leaves. There are a number of possible causes, the most likely being it's parched. If the soil looks and feels as dry as the Gobi Desert, your plant is in serious need of water. Put it in the sink or shower and let the water run through the soil; leave it in over the drain until the excess water runs out. It should revive within a few hours.

Ironically enough, another possible cause is too much water, recognizable when that same soil touch test leaves a muddy residue on your finger. Lay off the can for a few days.

Check the plant thoroughly for pests—fine spiderwebs, or bugs under the leaves or on the stems—as they can also cause droopy foliage.

If you're convinced it's none of the above, you might have a root problem. Spread out some newspaper and gently remove the plant from its container. Brush dirt from the root system until you can get a close-up look. If the roots look black and rotted, you've probably got root rot, caused by overwatering; if they're so tightly entwined it looks like the inside of a baseball, it's root-bound; if there are white or brown patches, there's a pest problem. If it's root-bound, you need to dig in your thumbs to break up the roots a little, then repot it in a larger container. If it's one of the other root problems, you should cut off the diseased sections (and spray with insecticidal soap if it's a pest problem) and put it back in the pot with some fresh dirt. It might take a few days to recover from the root shock. Don't worry, it should bounce back as soon as new roots form.

Brown and Withered Tips

Most common in plants with long thin leaves, this is could be caused by too much sun, not enough water, damage from being brushed by passersby, or from a lack of humidity. Make sure it's getting the right kind of light and check the soil for dryness. If it's in a heavily trafficked area, move it. Otherwise, increase the humidity by spritzing it or putting it on a tray of pebbles and water (see chapter 1, page 9).

Curling Leaves

Sap-sucking pests will often dry up the leaves, causing them to shrivel in exhaustion and self-defense. Check the tops and undersides of leaves for stickiness or the pests themselves and if you find anything, refer to the pest section below. If the leaves seem clean, the curling could be caused by dry soil or a lack of humidity.

TIP: Nature's Pest Repellents

For some reason, marigolds repel many of the pests that can destroy plants, especially vegetables. Plant a few in your tomato or pepper container to keep disease-ridden pests at bay.

Falling Foliage
Like people, plants can go into shock when faced with radical conditions. A dramatic temperature change or new light conditions can cause them to lose leaves, so try to keep the atmosphere consistent. On the other hand, your plant might be entering its dormant period (generally in the fall), in which case the loss of a few leaves is quite normal.

Holey Leaves
Hungry pests will gradually eat their way through your plants. Check the leaves thoroughly, then refer to the pest section below.

Buds Won't Flower
The budding/flowering process is a delicate one and a lot of things can make it go awry. Check the leaves for pests, which could be diverting the plant's attention from flowering to survival. Irregular watering, insufficient humidity, and temperature shifts can also botch bud development. Also consider that the vast majority of flowering plants need a healthy dose of sunlight, so make sure it's getting enough.

Loss of Leaf Color
Most plants, especially those with multicolor leaves, need sunlight to keep the color vibrant. Clip off the paling leaves and make sure the plant is getting enough sun.

Diseases 101
Since most plant disease is caused by neglect, this is where you can legitimately indulge in self-flagellation. But don't wallow in self-pity. The quicker you take action, the greater the chances for survival. Here are a few of the most common houseplant afflictions and how to cope.

Blackleg

It may sound like a pirate affliction, but in fact it's caused by over-watering. When the excess water sits for too long, it can literally rot away the stem. The disease generally starts where the main stem meets the soil and spreads up and down, turning the entire stem black.

It's a pretty insidious disease and once you've got it almost impossible to get rid of. Take cuttings from above the rot line and try to salvage some offspring.

Gray Mold

Generally caused by high humidity and low temperatures, it covers the leaves and stems of the plant in a gray, fluffy mold. You can avoid it by not allowing water to collect and remain on the leaves. Cut away the infected parts of the plant and reduce watering.

Mildew

Not unlike athlete's foot, mildew is caused by a fungus. It can be bought on by overwatering, poor air circulation, or too much humidity. White and powdery, it looks like the month-old cheese you forgot to wrap. Treat it the way you would gray mold. Cut away the infected areas and spray the rest of the plant with an antifungal solution, which you should be able to pick up at your local nursery.

Sooty Mold

Since this black moldy stuff attaches itself to the sap secreted by pests, it's a pretty good indication that you've got an infestation of some sort. It looks like soot and feels sticky and, though it doesn't directly do harm, it can clog the plant's pores and prevent light from reaching the leaves. To get rid of it, cut away the infected parts and wash the plant in soapy water.

Stem Rot

A soft, mushy stem and rotting leaves are a pretty good indication that your plant has stem rot. Caused most commonly by too much water, stem rot will literally eat the plant away from the inside. There is no real cure for it; the only possible way to save the infected plant is to cut away the infected part of the stem (if it hasn't reached below soil level) and hope the remaining portions form new growth.

Call the Exterminator

Pests can wreak havoc on your plant's life, eating leaves, sucking sap, and rotting the stems and roots. In small numbers, they're unlikely to be more than a nuisance, but they can multiply quickly so it's best to keep an eye out for them and kill them off before they call for reinforcements.

Some pretty obvious signs that you might have a pest problem are: tiny spider webs between the stems; mold on the leaves or stems; stunted growth; white powdery buildup on the leaves; or stickiness on the leaves, especially the underside. Some other indications are curling or falling leaves, holes in the foliage, and buds that won't flower (but check first to make sure the problem isn't caused by poor growing conditions, as discussed on pages 120–122). As soon as you discover an infestation, isolate the victim from any other plants to stop the pests from spreading.

Depending on what species is wreaking havoc with your plant, there are various ways to zap the critters. Insecticidal soaps do a good job of getting rid of most pests, and they're less toxic to the plant than a pure insecticide (though sometimes, the more persistent pests might call for all-out insecticide war). Choose your weapon and spritz it gently on the leaves—without soaking them—every week until you get rid of the problem.

Sometimes, the more persistent pests might call for all-out insecticide war.

TIP: Killer Insecticides

Though few things are more frustrating than the infestation of a carefully tended plant, don't go hog-wild with the toxic chemicals right off the bat. First try washing the leaves in lukewarm water. If that doesn't work, reach for the insecticidal soap.

When frustration hits and you need something stronger, start with the least toxic chemical compound. The gentler it is, the less likely you are to harm the plant.

Before you go splurging on insecticidal soap, try your own homemade version. Mix a few drops of gentle dishwashing soap with a quart of water. Pour the concoction in a spray bottle and spritz away.

TIP: It's All in the Application

The technique you use to apply the insecticide will depend on the type you're using and what you're trying to accomplish. Most will call for spraying. In that case, take the plant to a well-ventilated spot and spritz the entire plant, including the underside of leaves. Don't douse it, however, or its pores will be breathing insecticide for the next month.

Some brands call for a root application, in which case you'd add the recommended amount to the water and pour it on the soil as you normally would. Pesticides in powdered form are often sprinkled across the roots, where they are released gradually with each successive watering. Others come in the form of a spike, which you poke into the potting mixture. Whatever you use, make sure to first read the instructions.

Some pests go straight into the soil, calling for an insecticide to go directly into the pot. Read the directions on the container carefully to find out how much and often to use it.

The Major Culprits

Nom de Guerre: Aphids

With the lovely nickname of "plant lice," aphids are one of the uglier plant pests. They're little green bugs that suck sap and leave their white casings behind.

Signs of Destruction: Infected plants will be sticky, possibly with signs of white mold on the leaves. Also look for the white skeletons. They're disease-carriers so it's important to get rid of them as quickly as possible.

Best Weapons: Wash the plant thoroughly—stick it in the shower and rinse each of the leaves. Keep an eye on the plant and pick off bugs whenever you see them.

Nom de Guerre: Earthworms

Long and slimy, they're usually earthtoned in color.

Signs of Destruction: In the outdoor garden, they're a good thing, aerating the soil and adding nutrients with their feeding habits, but in a pot they can wreak havoc by loosening the soil and leaving their shed skins behind.

Best Weapons: Tap on the side of the pot to force them out of the soil. Then pick out all the worms you see and repot the plant, making sure to check the roots and soil thoroughly for any you might have missed.

Nom de Guerre: Earwigs

Brown and about an inch long, they look somewhat like a lobster with pincers in the back.

Signs of Destruction: Earwigs chew through leaves, leaving gaping holes, or, if they're allowed to take their own sweet time, mere leaf skeletons behind. They will also attack flowers.

Best Weapons: Using gloves (yes, those pincers do work), pick off any earwigs you see loitering on the leaves. Then wash the plant with insecticidal soap.

Nom de Guerre: Mealybugs

Up to a quarter inch long, mealybugs are fuzzy-looking oval sap suckers generally covered in a whitish secretion.

Signs of Destruction: They'll suck the life out of your plants' leaves, often causing them to curl or fall off. They also leave behind a sticky residue.

Best Weapons: Remove the obvious ones with a toothpick or cotton swab dipped in alcohol. Spray the leaves with insecticidal soap.

Nom de Guerre: Scale

Looking like little brown dots, scale insects tend to congregate in the crevices on the undersides of leaves.

Signs of Destruction: These sap-suckers leave a sticky residue so thick you might find some on surrounding surfaces. Infected leaves might curl up in self-defense or fall off.

Best Weapons: They're tough to get rid of and you're best off starting with a cotton swab, some alcohol, and a lot of patience. Clean the leaves carefully, scraping off the scale with your fingernail or the swab, then spritz with insecticidal soap.

Nom de Guerre: Spider Mites

These tiny little red spiders would almost be cute if they weren't such a destructive pain. They leave behind a fine spiderweb in the crooks between leaves.

Signs of Destruction: The fine webs are a surefire indication of spider mites. Other signs are yellowing and falling leaves, blackened flower buds, and stunted growth.

Best Weapons: Wash the leaves thoroughly to get rid of existing spiders. And since they thrive in hot, dry air, misting might help stave them off. In severe cases spray with insecticidal soap or insecticide.

TIP: Avoiding a Plague

After you've isolated the sick plant, examine any others that were in contact with it for signs of the same pests or disease. If you see anything, even the tiniest, most isolated spider mite, separate that plant out too. The sooner you deal with potential infestation, the better your chances of licking it before every green thing in your home begins to droop and drop leaves.

Nom de Guerre: Thrips

Though only a fraction of an inch long, thrips look like miniature flies, though they're more inclined to leap.

Signs of Destruction: Basically sap-suckers, thrips feed on foliage and flowers, leaving behind white patches surrounded by black specks.

Best Weapons: Shaking the plant over a white sheet of paper will flush out large numbers of them. Then spray with a mild insecticide or wash the leaves with insecticidal soap.

Nom de Guerre: Weevils

Difficult to miss, weevils are about a half inch long and look like small beetles.

Signs of Destruction: Weevils feed on the foliage and chew away at the roots of the plant, sometimes to the point where there are no roots left.

Best Weapons: Remove any surfacing weevils by hand, then treat the root system with a mild insecticide.

Nom de Guerre: Whiteflies

Truly annoying and very difficult to get rid of, whiteflies are just that—tiny white flies that tend to congregate on the underside of leaves and suck away at the sap. If you suspect you have them, tap at a few leaves; if you see a cloud of white, you've got them.

Signs of Destruction: The leaves will curl up and turn yellow and flower buds blacken and die. They also secrete a sticky sap and lay multitudes of little white eggs so you can have generations of infestation.

Best Weapons: Repeated sprayings with insecticidal soap or insecticide—every few days or so—will usually work over time. Wash the leaves as often as possible, concentrating on the undersides, to get rid of eggs.

TIP: Desperate Moves

If you've tried and failed to get rid of pests like whiteflies or spider mites, you might want to turn the vacuum on them. Using the hose of your cleaner and keeping suction as low as possible, brush it across the underside of leaves, obviously trying to avoid taking the whole plant with the pests.

index

Index

Index